murders
of Hull

Highgate of Beverley

Highgate Publications (Beverley) Limited
1996

murders
of Hull

The research and writing of this book has been
no one-man achievement.
My thanks for their help and co-operation in
this project go to Brian Jones, Liz Howell, Anne
Lightfoot, Brian Mitchell, Chris Ketchell, the
staff at Donald Innes Photographers, Mrs C.
Jessop and Malcom Young.
Above all, my thanks and love to Alison for her
encouragement, support and endless supplies
of patience.

Angus Young

MURDERS OF HULL

British Library Cataloguing in Publication Data.
A catalogue record for this book is available from the British Library.

© Hull Daily Mail Publications Limited, 1995
First edition published by Quality Publications, Hull Daily Mail Publications Limited,
1995

ISBN 0 948929 91 X

Published by

Highgate of Beverley

Highgate Publications (Beverley) Limited
24 Wylies Road, Beverley, HU17 7AP
Telephone (01482) 866826

Produced by

4 Newbegin, Lairgate, Beverley, HU17 8EG
Telephone (01482) 886017

INTRODUCTION

Murder undoubtedly remains the most fascinating of crimes. By its very nature, the act of taking another life is extraordinary.

This book looks at some of the more remarkable murder cases in the Hull area for over a 100 year period, from the brutal killing of a young apprentice on a fishing smack which shocked Victorian England to Bruce Lee's deadly series of fatal fires in the 1970s.

The cases offer examples of human tragedy, expert detective work and courtroom drama. Having reported on several murder investigations and subsequent trials, I know at first hand the emotions they stir.

CONTENTS

MURDERS OF HULL

THE MURDER OF A FISHERBOY

✝

O n December 16 1881, the wooden fishing smack Rising Sun left Albert Dock destined for the Dogger Bank. The six-man crew would be away from home over Christmas but a profitable return on the catch would be their compensation. Necessity was more important than seasonal sentiment to Hull's fishing fleet of the day. Joseph Papper knew that more than most. A coal merchant, his son William had always fancied a life at sea. By the time he was 13, the young Papper was apprenticed to Osmond Otto Brand, the 27-year-old owner of the Rising Sun and an admired skipper.

Brought up helping his father's coal business, Papper was a strong lad for his size and well used to hard physical work. Healthy and sharp-witted, he was ideal for his role as a teenage workhorse on board the smack. Between voyages he lived not with the parents but at Brand's house on Hessle Road, a common practice among fisherboys serving what was usually a seven-year apprenticeship with a skipper.

At 14, Papper was the youngest of three apprentices on board the Rising Sun that day. He was officially the cook for the trip but was literally expected to pull his weight in the tough job of hauling up the smack's trawl by hand. As soon as fish were caught, they would be packed in ice and stored until the cargo was sufficient to return home.

In his eight months under Brand, Papper had worked hard and the crew knew him as an amiable lad who was always highly regarded by his skipper. But with just one remark as he boarded the Rising Sun that day, things were to change dramatically and Papper would never be seen by his family again.

As the boy arrived at the smack as it prepared to sail, Brand was with his wife on the dockside. Papper approached the couple and declared: "Skipper, my sister Emma says she knows you".

Whether they were the words of a 14-year-old boy innocently repeating an equally innocuous remark made previously by his elder sister or whether they referred to something more serious was never properly established. But having been uttered in earshot of his wife, they were enough to enrage Brand and effectively condemn Papper to death.

Within minutes of setting sail, a furious Brand told the boy: "I'll pay for you when I get you out of the dock.". Turning to one of the crew, the skipper added: "He has been telling my wife a lot of lies about me respecting his sister".

Papper denied lying but this only enraged Brand even more. When the boat dropped anchor for the first night off Sunk Island, Brand told the boy to go below to fetch some reef lacing and followed him into the cabin. Initially, out of sight of the rest of the crew, Brand started to thrash the lad with a knotted rope which had an iron thimble at each end. Papper's cries eventually alerted the boat's second hand, William Dench, who went below only to see Brand chasing the boy around the cabin.

Another apprentice, William Blackburn, who was five years older than Papper, also witnessed part of that first beating and would later claim the skipper shouted at his victim: "I have done your sister and I will do you".

A second beating followed later that night using the same length of rope, establishing a pattern of regular daily assaults against the boy by the skipper which continued until three days before Christmas when Brand's campaign of cruelty reached new heights.

Now on the Dogger Bank, some 90 miles from Spurn Point, the crew were hauling the trawl that morning when Brand, seemingly without any provocation, stepped up to Papper and punched him squarely in the face, knocking the lad to the deck before telling him: "Go forward and stop there for three days".

The order effectively meant Papper had to spend the next 72 hours on deck. To make matters worse, Brand then ordered him to stand on the boat's stem and stay there for two hours.

Usually a short plank at the bow of a boat where the hull joins to a point, the stem would have been a dangerous place to stand even in calm weather but this was in the depths of winter in the North Sea. As it happened, the weather at the time was calm but the sea swell still made the vessel roll heavily.

Lying on the floor half-dazed from the punch and crying, Papper initially refused to obey the order but Brand got hold of a bucket and began throwing freezing water over the boy until he relented. Once in position, his torment continued as he was forced to hold onto the boat's rail with one hand and, under instruction from his skipper, began singing at the top of his voice: "If I had not been a bad lad I should not have been here, cuckoo''.

Humiliated, shivering from his soaked clothes and in danger of falling into the sea at any moment, the boy stayed on the stem for two hours despite Brand and another crew member, Frederick Rycroft, throwing mud pellets at him made from the debris dredged up in the trawl from the bottom of the sea.

With Papper still on the stem, the crew retired for breakfast and on Brand's return he was found lying exhausted on the deck, barely able to move or speak. This didn't stop Brand from throwing more buckets of water over him before thrashing him again with his favoured length of rope, tipped with iron thimbles.

On Christmas Eve, the beatings and the soakings continued as Papper remained on deck. At one stage, Brand wrapped the rope around the boy's neck, pulled both ends and nearly choked him. The skipper then jumped on the boy's stomach before dragging him to the halyard rope used to hoist lanterns aloft during fishing.

The worst fears of the watching crew were realised when Brand placed the halyard rope around the boy's neck and chest and ordered Blackburn to winch him up. The horrified young apprentice initially did nothing but Brand threatened to hang him, too, and Papper was slowly hoisted up, too weak to make a struggle of it.

With Brand holding his legs to steady him, the boy rose over five feet above the deck before the supporting crosstrees yardarm broke and Papper tumbled back onto the deck, almost senseless. When Blackburn pointed out that Papper had nearly been hung, Brand snapped back: "Oh bugger the lad, the crosstrees are the worst".

The accident only seemed to infuriate Brand even more. Unable to walk, the boy was in no condition to obey an order to move forward again and instead began crawling pathetically across the deck. As he did so, Brand kicked him and then jumped on him. As the boat rolled, the weakened boy rolled onto his back and was jumped on again before being soaked by yet another bucket of water.

The order to move forward not only kept Papper on deck but also, in the eyes of Brand at least, kept him away from the dinner table. Apart from the physical beatings he was also being starved to death.

Over his three days on deck, Papper was only officially allowed water and broken biscuits but even these were rationed by Brand. While the skipper was asleep, the crew would give him food but at one point the boy was reduced to eating a raw skate from part of the catch. Under normal circumstances, Papper might have been expected to cook the crew's Christmas Day dinner. As it was, he remained on deck as they tucked into two ducks, a piece of roast beef, potatoes and plum pudding.

Eventually, Brand called him near the cabin, put some pudding on a fork and held it out to him. As the boy reached out, the skipper rapped him across the knuckles with a stick and then fed him a single currant stuck on his fork. Once the duck bones had been picked by the men, Brand gave them first to the ship's dog before Papper was allowed the remains. The boy's subsequent pitiful request for a fresh biscuit was then refused.

It seems the order for Papper to remain on deck was stretched beyond Christmas Day with the crew wrapping him in the foresail at night to keep him warm. Yet despite his condition, he was still expected to work.

The beatings and the bullying from Brand continued. On Boxing Day he threw an 18lb lead weight overboard and ordered the boy to pull it in five times an hour. With the smack sailing at the time and the line pulled tight, the task was beyond the weakened teenager, who had earlier struggled to even clear the crew's breakfast table. When Brand went below, the crew pulled in the line and later told the skipper that Papper had carried out his order. The boy's reward, albeit 24 hours later, was a single dumpling after being promised a "good dinner".

On the 28th, Papper told his skipper he felt dirty and ill, perhaps hoping he would be allowed to go below and wash and put on a fresh pair of clothes. Brand had other ideas and ordered the boy to be washed on deck in a tub usually used for storing freshly-caught fish. On the skipper's orders, he was then hauled out naked and dragged around the deck to dry with Dench and Rycroft holding an arm each. Afterwards, the boy was given new clothing but was so weak he could not even pull on his socks, provoking yet another furious beating by Brand who sent him back on deck only half-dressed.

Over a week of sickening cruelty reached its unsavoury climax on the following day, December 29, and it was sparked by Papper defying the order to remain on deck because of the call of nature.

The crew used a bucket kept below in the hold as a toilet and while Papper struggled to keep some sort of dignity his absence from the deck was spotted by Rycroft and immediately reported to Brand.

The skipper ordered the lad to be hauled back on deck with a rope which was tied under his arms. Once hauled through the hatchway the familiar beatings began again. At one point, Rycroft emptied the contents of the bucket Papper had been sitting on into his mouth and smeared it across his face. Papper was then lashed by both hands to the rail and again soaked with water. As the boat's fog bell sounded, Brand told him: "The bell is tolling for your death. You'll not live another day in this ship."

Somehow, Papper wriggled free but was soon found cowering in the fo'c'sle. Brand then ordered him to be thrown in the dill, the space between the floor of the fo'c'sle and the bottom of the boat. When the floorboards were taken up and Dench saw the dill contained at least three feet of water, he refused to obey his skipper's order, which included nailing down the floorboards again. An experienced fisherman, he knew Brand had gone too far.

Rycroft, however, had no hesitation. Putting a rope under the boy's arms, he shoved him in and then stood aside as Brand began standing on Papper's shoulders as he sat in the dill with the water up to his chest. After ten minutes, Dench persuaded Brand to haul him out but the lad's suffering was not over yet. As Dench and the third apprentice Yates pulled him out, Brand beat him with a stick and then floored him again with a punch which sent blood spurting from his nose. Even then the skipper was not finished, raining further blows and kicks on the groaning boy as he lay helpless on the deck.

Papper never properly regained consciousness again. Brand laughed off the crew's fears that the boy was dying, telling them: "A bloody good job, too!" before tucking into his dinner. Instead, he believed Papper was trying to trick him. His belated attempts to revive him, by first hanging him overboard while stitched into a piece of canvas and then shoving tobacco and tea down his throat, only hastened the boy's death. Once dead, the boy's body was placed in a cabin bunk and Brand began covering his crime. First, he decided that David Yates, the third apprentice and the only crew member not to have witnessed Papper's last moments, could not be trusted to stay silent if told the truth. A plot was then hatched to make it look as though Papper had accidentally been knocked overboard during the night by one of the sails caught in a gust of wind.

Infact, as Yates slept, the body had been tossed into the sea nearly three hours before the bogus cry of "Papper's overboard" went up.

Brand knew he dare not take the body back to Hull and then claim his apprentice had died in an accident. The injuries he had inflicted told another story. With Yates still believing Papper had been knocked overboard and lost, the skipper decided to carry on fishing for another two days before heading for Hull on New Year's Day. To avoid questions over the delay in his return to port, he then ordered the crew to say Papper had been lost on January 1.

The boy's father was at the dockside when the Rising Sun arrived back on January 5. A grim-faced Brand broke the news that his son had been knocked overboard by the boat's foresail and offered the distraught man a glass of whisky. Brand then made his way to the police station in Parliament Street and made a brief statement recording the death.

It read: "I report that at about 5.30am on January 1 1882, we were trawling on the fishing ground about 120 miles from Spurn, when the cook, William Papper, 14 years of age, a native of Hull, was knocked overboard (and drowned) by the big foresail sheet. The smack was put about and every effort was made to save him, but without avail."

Deaths of fisherboys at sea were not uncommon at the time. In 1881, no fewer than 22 apprentices from Hull failed to return home, most reported as being washed overboard from their smacks.

With the crew intimidated into supporting his story, Brand might have thought he was in the clear but doubts remained in the Papper family, who went with their uncertainties, being quoted in newspapers as claiming that Brand had beaten young William. Brand responded by making another statement to the police at his own home, asking Blackburn and Yates, who were with him in the room at the time, if Papper had been well treated. They both agreed he had.

The police decided to take no action and, as Brand and his crew returned to sea, a veil of silence fell over he affair which was to last nearly two months.

After two further trips under Brand, his apprentices Blackburn and Yates could not stand the lies anymore and visited the home of Hull's Chief Constable, James Campbell, to make a partial statement revealing the truth behind Papper's death. They gave further statements the following day, along with Dench who had also kept dutifully quiet until then.

Brand and Rycroft were arrested and charged with murder and as details of the charges emerged, it caused a sensation. Varying accounts of the fateful fishing trip began to find their way into print. Similarly, pamphlets appeared featuring illustrations of Brand beating the lad before the case had even reached a trial. Witnesses among the crew were taken into police custody for their own protection and when the trial of the two men did begin at Leeds Assizes, the courtroom was packed with spectators who had queued for hours to get the best seats.

The murder charge against Rycroft was quickly thrown out and the jury was ordered to find him guilty of inflicting bodily harm and common assault. Brand pleaded not guilty to murder and sat silently as first Dench then Blackburn and Yates delivered their damning evidence, his seemingly calm appearance betrayed by constantly twisting his fingers together.

With 14 years' experience at sea, Dench's evidence carried most weight. He told the court he had previously witnessed boys being bullied, beaten with ropes, punched and even kept without dinner. "That was a common kind of punishment on board smacks," he said. But Papper's treatment at the hands of Brand had been different to other apprentices. "I have never before seen them come in for such rough usage," he added.

To some extent, the crew were also on trial even though they faced no criminal charges. They stood accused, by the defence at least, of meekly obeying orders and doing nothing to help save the boy's life. They replied by painting Brand as a sadistic monster who ruled by fear and who kept a loaded revolver in his bunk, firing it once at Rycroft on the return journey.

Brand, who was hissed and booed by spectators at every adjournment, did not give evidence but in his original brief, statements to the police had sought to spread the blame to the rest of the crew. "I did not do it, there are four others in it besides me," he said

The jury took just seven minutes to find him guilty of murder. Passing the death sentence, Mr Justice Watkin Williams told Brand: "In all my personal experience and from all my reading of the state of crime in this country, I have never read a crime of greater atrocity than that of which the jury have convicted you."

As he was led back to the cells to a chorus of hisses from the court gallery, Brand defiantly swore and shook his fist at the crowd and later unsuccessfully tried to escape from the cab taking him to nearby Armley Jail, being grabbed by a prison warder after forcing open a door.

A huge crowd had gathered outside the court in Leeds for the verdict and some of these later attempted to storm the lodgings used by the Rising Sun's crew during the trial in an attempt to lynch Dench. They were turned away by a brave police sergeant but a similar lynch party later turned up at Dench's home in Hull only for their intended victim to escape through a rear window.

Brand maintained his innocence to the end, writing a final letter claiming he alone did not kill the boy. He was hanged at Armley Jail on May 23 1882.

Papper's murder, together with the similar murder of another Hull fisherboy at sea two months later, caused a scandal and prompted an investigation into the fishing industry's apprentice system which had long been tainted by accusations of exploitation and cruelty.

Nine years earlier William Donker, an 18-year-old Hull apprentice, jumped overboard and drowned after continual beatings by his skipper William Brussey, and in 1880 284 fisherboy apprentices were sent to prison in Hull for deserting their ships.

The Board of Trade inquiry reviewed legislation covering fisherboys but it was the growth of large fishing firms at the expense of family-owned smacks towards the end of the 19th century that eventually signalled the demise of the old apprentice system.

The legacy of the Papper case lived on, however, in Hull's fishing community, partly through a number of poems and folk songs written about his death and Brand's fate at the gallows. One verse ended:

"So all you brave Captains that plough the deep sea,
Just think of these words written by me,
Treat your boys well and kindness employ,
Don't let them meet with the fate of the poor 'prentice boy".

THE BLACK FLAG FLIES AGAIN

✝

he student of human nature would have found much food for thought moving about in this crowd, noting the stamp of countenance, marking the character of speech, listening to the sentiments expressed. He would have been struck by the prevailing callousness and unconcern; and he would have been startled perhaps by much ribaldry. The impending doom of the man now at the threshold of the scaffold was discussed with light-hearted freedom by many a hard-faced labourer." These words belong to an anonymous sketchwriter witnessing a piece of history unfolding before his eyes outside the gates of Hull Prison. Inside the jail, 30-year-old Arthur Richardson was about to become the first man to be executed in Hull for over 100 years. It was March 1902 and the cold, wet and bleak day which marked the occasion only added to the grim spectacle.

The earliest recorded mention of the death penalty in Hull is contained in Edward I's Royal Charter of 1299, which marked the handover of the town to the King from a powerful group of land-owning monks. In the Charter, Edward pledges to build a prison "for the punishment of evil-doers" in his newly-acquired borough as well as a set of gallows just outside the town but on his own land. The King appointed his own warden to effectively run the town and make sure his laws were obeyed and the plans for a prison and gallows were a natural extension of this. The Charter succinctly explains this by stating the measures were there "so that the aforementioned warden may execute judgement".

In 1302 a gibbet was built just outside the new town boundary north-west of Beverley Gate where the roads to Beverley and Cottingham divided, probably where Jameson Street is today. One of the earliest maps of Hull, believed to be drawn in Elizabethan times but depicting the town in 1350, clearly shows this gibbet outside the walls in open country.

Another gibbet followed later, fixed above the entrance to the town at Beverley Gate while gallows were also used near the banks of the Humber in what is now West Dock Street.

In the 16th century, the Court of Quarter Sessions in Hull had the power of life and death and frequently chose the latter. Men were executed for sheep stealing, theft, forgery and burglary. This bloodletting continued until 1778 when John Rogerson became the last man to be publicly executed in Hull.

Rogerson had been in trouble since boyhood, first stealing a hamper of gingerbread from a house at the age of nine. By the time he was 15 he was living on his wits, travelling across the country to various fairs and stealing to survive. One of the criminal skills he picked up along the way was coining, or counterfeiting money, regarded by the authorities as an act of high treason and punishable by death.

Originally from Lincolnshire, he arrived in Hull after being acquitted of the theft of goods belonging to a breeches-maker near his home village of Kerton. In reality he had been involved and simply returned to a haystack where the haul had been stashed after his trial and headed for Hull.

Here his coining skills let him down and he was arrested, the stolen breeches turning up in a search of his room, but Rogerson then escaped from jail in a daring break-out with several other prisoners and went on the run. He briefly enlisted in the Army in Liverpool but soon deserted and was eventually re-arrested in Wakefield for another offence of coining before being brought back to Hull.

Sentenced to death, he was visited by the Rev George Lambert, the first minister of the Fish Street chapel which stood near the prison.

"I waited on him in his dungeon, conversed with him for some time and found him very ignorant of the way of salvation and flattering himself with the hopes of a pardon or at least a mitigation of the sentence," wrote Rev Lambert later.

The minister remained a regular visitor and accompanied Rogerson, at the prisoner's own request, to the execution in Gallows Lane, where Great Thornton Street is today. Rogerson was taken there on a horse-drawn wooden sledge, being pulled through streets packed with spectators.

Rev Lambert wrote: "He walked down the stairs with as much composure as if he was going to liberty and stepped into the sledge on which lay his coffin as if it had been a coach to take him upon to visit a friend".

On arriving at the gallows, the minister recalled Rogerson's "unshaken firmness" and, with the noose around his neck, noted he was "frequently signifying his desire to be gone by putting one foot down from the place on which he stood".

Rogerson reportedly delivered a speech and confession to the large crowd which had assembled moments before he was hanged, although it is likely most, if not all, of it was actually written and read by Rev Lambert. Its eloquence and tone, including passages warning of the evils of bad company, breaking the Sabbath and being disobedient to one's parents, seems at odds with most of Rogerson's short life. He was just 26 when, in the words of the clergyman at his side, he was "sent from our world either with a general groan or a cry for mercy from the numerous spectators". The execution would be the last in Hull for 124 years, with subsequent hangings being carried out either in York or Leeds usually depending on where the offenders' trial was held.

A change in the law at the dawn of the 20th century brought the death sentence back to Hull, enabling executions to be carried out inside the city's prison on Hedon Road, the grisly spectacle of public hangings having been brought to an end in Britain in 1868.

Like Rogerson, Arthur Richardson would achieve lasting notoriety for the punishment he received rather than for the crime he committed.

Born in Hull and a joiner by trade, he signed up with the Army and served in India until his late twenties when he left the military and returned to England to marry. The marriage was not a success and the couple soon separated with Richardson moving to Brigg in Lincolnshire, where he had an aunt.

His relative in the bustling market town soon had good reason to rue her nephew's arrival as he proceeded to rob her of £26. He was arrested almost immediately and sentenced to six months' imprisonment in Lincoln Jail.

Released in November 1901, he returned to Hull virtually penniless with the intention of seeing his wife. He took lodgings with a couple called Skelton, telling them he had a job at the nearby Reckitt's factory. In his first week there, the Skeltons hardly ever saw their new lodger as he was out of the house shortly after 5am every morning, presumably setting off early to start his shift.

But one woman was dreading seeing Richardson. Mrs Sarah Hebden was a widow who lived on her own in Hodgson Street in East Hull. Despite being 60 years old, she still worked as an insurance agent for the Royal Liver Friendly Society and collected payments from friends and neighbours, earning a weekly commission of around £2. It was a useful income and, combined with her careful nature when it came to money, she not only owned her own property but also enjoyed a healthy bank balance.

For years, Mrs Hebden had kept a little of her own money in a tea caddy hidden in her bedroom. One of the few people who knew of its existence was her nephew, Arthur Richardson. As a boy, Richardson had been a frequent visitor to his aunt's house and knew her habits only too well. His mother still lived next door.

THE BLACK FLAG FLIES AGAIN

Mrs Hebden was last seen alive on the evening of November 27, the day before a planned trip to Elloughton. The next day there was no answer from her door and a check with the Royal Liver Friendly Society's offices revealed she had failed to call in as expected. Her worried sister next door sent her own daughter, Florence, to investigate as dusk fell. The police were called when her flickering candlelight picked out the body of her aunt lying sprawled on the floor near to the foot of the stairs'.

The police were greeted with a ghastly sight. Two large pools of blood covered the floor and one of Mrs Hebden's fingers had nearly been ripped off. Lying near her badly battered head were a pair of blood-drenched tongs, twisted and bent by the force of the attack. The post-mortem would later reveal she had been struck about 20 blows to the head and had died around 6am that morning.

Upstairs in her bedroom the tea caddy had been opened. Inside were two empty purses and a newspaper cutting of Richardson's conviction for the robbery of his aunt in Brigg. Mrs Hebden's fears about her nephew had been realised.

As was his habit, Richardson had left his lodgings early that morning. He was next seen on Holderness Road at 7.30am, telling a friend that he had struck lucky with a bet and was off to spend his winnings. Giving a false name and address, he went on to order a new suit and bought himself an overcoat, new collars and ties.

No-one was more surprised by this transformation than his landlords, the Skeltons, who had assumed Richardson had little or no money. When asked about his new clothes, he claimed they were to impress his wife and then showed them another new acquisition, a gold watch. With details of his aunt's death in the newspapers, he unexpectedly returned to his lodgings during the following morning apparently distraught, claiming he had discovered the news from a colleague at Reckitt's. Later that day he continued to grieve for his aunt fairly loudly in a local pub.

The police arrested him two days after finding the body. In his room they found blood-stained clothing which had been recently washed, a bank book belonging to Mrs Hebden as well as a woman's brooch and a silk handkerchief.

Nonetheless, Richardson protested his innocence. The money for his new clothes, he said, had come from a £10 note he had concealed while in Lincoln Prison. He claimed the watch had been pawned in Grimsby where he had also bought the brooch while the handkerchief spotted with blood was from a shaving accident. Without the forensic knowledge of today, the case against him was entirely circumstantial as no-one had actually been seen at the widow's house but it was still overwhelming.

At his trial in York, Richardson pleaded not guilty to murder but set the tone for his defence by supplying messages scribbled on prison notepaper to his barrister who had little else to rely on in presenting his case.

Richardson's own evidence from the witness box only served to condemn him even further. After initially telling police he left his house at 7am on the morning of his aunt's death, he admitted in court he had lied but claimed he could not remember his movements that morning. He also changed his story about the watch. He told the jury his aunt had given it to him two days before her death, asking him to repair it for her. The bloodstains, he said, came from nosebleeds and a fight with a stranger on the day of his arrest. He also belatedly owned up to never having worked at Reckitt's, saying he invented the story to convince the Skeltons he had money to pay his rent. Ironically, among the jury was the prominent Hull industrialist Sir James Reckitt, no doubt relieved to discover the man in the dock was not one of his employees after all.

When Richardson said his remark about winning a bet had simply been a joke, the patience of Judge Justice Lawrence finally snapped and he warned him: "For heaven's sake, think of what you are saying. Do think what position you are standing in!"

Richardson only proved himself to be a consummate liar and the jury took just 20 minutes to find him guilty as charged. Asked by the court clerk if he had anything to say, he declared: "All that I have to say is that I am innocent, and whatever punishment I receive is unjust".

With the death sentence duly passed, he continued to show no sign of remorse and arriving back in Hull he flashed a smile at the waiting crowd in Paragon Station as he stepped off the train flanked by two prison officers.

The gallows which awaited him at Hull Prison were capable of hanging three men at once but hadn't been installed there for Richardson. Infact, they had been built a year earlier for an execution which never took place. John Walker, who had stabbed his drunken father to death, escaped the noose after a successful appeal to the Home Secretary citing his age of 21 years as grounds for mercy.

Richardson was not so fortunate, despite the efforts of his mother who lodged an official appeal to reprieve him on the grounds of his stated innocence. She also pointed to changes in him since leaving the Army but the realistic chances of a reprieve were always going to be slim.

When confirmation came that Richardson was to hang, the responsibility for Hull's first execution in over a century fell to the city's Under-Sheriff, Alderman Arthur Rollit. One of his first decisions was to refuse the Press any access to the event.

It was not an altogether surprising move by the authorities. One of the main reasons for ending public executions 30 years earlier had been the growing criticism surrounding the actual act of hanging a condemned prisoner. Officially, death was supposed to be instantaneous but hangings were often bungled. Some prisoners were left being slowly choked to death while others were nearly decapitated simply because the hangman had miscalculated the drop needed to break the victim's neck. On other occasions, a body would remain twitching for up to 20 minutes.

Even after moving executions behind prison walls, they still caused controversy. The hanging of Hull man Vincent Walker at York Castle prison in 1878 was a typical example. Walker had stabbed a woman friend of his wife's 17 times in a furious rage and was sentenced to death for murder and, unfortunately for all concerned, the hangman gave Walker insufficient drop. Newspapers told their readers Walker "died very hard with as much as seven minutes elapsing before life was fully extinct".

THE BLACK FLAG FLIES AGAIN

The unease of Richardson's fate was also evident among Hull's own magistrates. By law, an execution had to be carried out in the presence of a magistrate but at a special meeting held to discuss the issue none of the justices felt inclined to carry out the duty. They agreed instead to hold a ballot but before the shortest straw was drawn, Dr George Lilley JP volunteered to spare his colleagues from further discomfort.

The hangman chosen to carry out the execution was William Billington, who was assisted by his younger brother John. They were the sons of James Billington, a barber from Bolton who began the family sideline in hanging. Billington senior carried out most of his work dressed entirely in black, complete with a black skull cap, and used his sons as assistants until they eventually succeeded him as executioners in their own right.

Arriving in Hull the day before the execution, the Billington brothers spent the night in the prison, visiting Richardson in his cell to measure him for the drop. As he was slightly built, a 10ft drop was agreed on and sandbags were used to test the strength of the rope destined to be placed around his neck.

Richardson reportedly slept well that night, rising at 6am the next morning to eat a good breakfast. The Prison Chaplain then visited him to offer Holy Communion before the Billington brothers entered the cell to strap his arms together. Officials including the prison governor, doctor and Deputy-Sheriff were present when Richardson at last confessed his guilt, stating: "I have made my peace with God and I believe I am forgiven, and I ask for the forgiveness of my fellow men".

Outside the prison gates a huge crowd had gathered to watch the large wall clock count down the condemned man's last minutes. A group of policemen stood on the pavement outside the main door and officers also kept guard outside the closed gates of the nearby cemetery to prevent spectators climbing trees for a better view. As well as the clock, all eyes were fixed on a flapping cord attached to a flagpole towering over the prison building.

The gallows had been erected just yards from Richardson's cell and the procession to them covered no more than ten paces. Standing on the scaffold, his legs were pinioned and then the rope was placed around his neck before a white hood was drawn over his head. William Billington quickly pulled a bolt and Richardson disappeared into a pit below, the rope twitching once as it reached its full length. The whole proceedings, from leaving the cell to the execution, had taken less than a minute. The inquest was told death had been instantaneous.

As the clock fingers told the waiting spectators the hour of execution had arrived, a hush fell over the crowd and a prison bell signalling the hanging rang out. The cord on the flagpole tightened and the black flag was raised, the signal of death by execution had returned to Hull.

Although the traditional use of the flag would soon be ended in England, the death bell at Hull Prison sounded nine more times over the next 32 years.

MURDERS OF HULL

THE SERIAL KILLER OF HESSLE ROAD

†

From Jack the Ripper to the Yorkshire Ripper, serial killers have fascinated both criminologists and the public alike. As the famous Whitechapel murders in Victorian London show, those who kill serially are not a recent phenomenon yet it was not until the 1970s that the first fully-fledged research programme was established to study the techniques of serial killers and detail the patterns that emerged. The findings by the American FBI's Behavioural Science Unit have been used to define serial killing ever since.

The study identified a variable set of elements, some or all of which are found in serial killers and distinguish them from single-incident murderers or other categories of multicide such as so-called 'spree murderers' like Michael Ryan, who shot 17 people dead in Hungerford in 1987.

One of the key characteristics in serial murder is the fact that the act is repeated over a period of time — sometimes years — and continues until the killer is put behind bars, dies or kills themselves.

That pattern only partially tells the story of Billy Burkitt, a man destined to rewrite this country's criminal record books. For Burkitt not only killed three times but in doing so dispatched three married women in almost identical circumstances in three different decades and remarkably escaped being hanged on each occasion.

Each offence was committed within the same tightly-knit neighbourhood of Hessle Road and the only reason for the long gaps in between was simply that he was serving a prison sentence for his previous crime at the time. The pattern of his killings only came to an end when he was finally jailed for life.

In August 1915, Burkitt was a 28-year-old and working as a fisherman, having recently carried out minesweeping duties off the East Coast. The First World War was beginning to grind to halt in the trenches in France and the horrors of the conflict were being felt in Hull as the bodies from the sunken British E-13 submarine were being brought back to the city from Copenhagen in Denmark.

Just 5ft 5ins tall and clean shaven, Burkitt looked younger than his age and undoubtedly had an eye for the ladies. He also had a jealous streak that would prove to be his downfall. That summer he was often seen with Mrs Mary Tyler, a married woman with two children who was also known as Polly. Mrs Tyler had lived apart from her husband Arthur, a private with the East Yorkshire Regiment, for several years and even though she shared her Derwent Terrace home with another fisherman called George Harding, Burkitt would visit her regularly when he was away.

In the middle of the month Burkitt returned to Hull after a spell sailing out of Scarborough and immediately began seeing Polly Tyler again. He made no secret of the relationship and neighbours in the densely-populated rows of terraces soon knew they were a couple who were fond of each other despite bursts of frequent quarrelling. Burkitt was undoubtedly jealous of the fact that his lover was still living with another man, albeit one whose absence at sea allowed their affair to carry on.

Despite regularly giving her money, Polly Tyler also had doubts about Burkitt's true affections and these surfaced when she discovered a photograph of him with his arm around a girl in Scarborough. He claimed it was an innocent snap and even disputed it was actually him in the picture. The couple argued on and off for two days, with Polly Tyler spending one night with a neighbour, telling her she was afraid of Burkitt after he had threatened to "do" her.

By Saturday August 28, the couple were back together again but George Harding was also due to return any day. Another row erupted in the early evening after both had been drinking. Burkitt would later tell police Mrs Tyler pulled off her wedding ring and threw it at him but his act hardly justified his response. He grabbed a pocketknife and stabbed her four times, twice in the neck. One of the blows pierced her jugular vein and she was dead within minutes, lying in a pool of blood on the kitchen floor.

Burkitt left immediately and walked to his mother's house in nearby Worcester Terrace, off Gillett Street. There he met his brother Harold, who was dumfounded when Burkitt handed him the bent pocketknife, his belt and a halfpenny which he asked to look after as a keepsake. He also noticed his brother's blood-stained hands. Their widowed mother Mary then arrived back at the house and was confronted by her son Billy shouting: "I have done it. I have done Polly in!" before running out into the street.

Mrs Burkitt knew of her son's stormy relationship and decided to find out what had happened herself. Arriving at Derwent Terrace, she found Burkitt standing on the street corner and she demanded he hand over the key. Along with a neighbour, she opened Mrs Tyler's front door and waited for Billy to light the gas and point out the body covered by a cloak in the corner of the kitchen.

"What have you done it for?" asked Mrs Burkitt but her son replied: "She will not tantalise anyone else now". The strange visiting party then left the house in darkness again and Burkitt ran off, claiming he was going to kill himself. The Tyler children, Flora and George, knew him well and that night came across him while making their way home from a trip to the cinema. He unexpectedly grabbed ten-year-old George, handed him a key and told them: "Take the first policeman you see to your house. Tell him your mother is dead."

By the time the youngsters and a constable had reached the house, a large crowd of neighbours were following in their footsteps. Among them was Harold Burkitt, who had heard Flora's cries and had realised the awful truth to what he first thought had been a joke by his brother.

The same constable who was led to the body of Mrs Tyler arrested her killer in the early hours of the next morning. Burkitt had spent the night curled up asleep inside a drain pipe, his suicide threat apparently having come to nothing. Woken up by the officer, he was marched to Gordon Street police station, declaring on the way: "She has brought me down to this, but she won't bring another bugger down".

An inquest heard post-mortem evidence which pointed to an attack of brutal violence. Two of the wounds were so deep that only considerable force could have been used to inflict them. Another stab wound had been checked by the woman's shoulder bone, accounting for the condition of the knife. There was also bruising found on her chin. In contrast, Burkitt had been unmarked when arrested.

All the evidence seemed to suggest only one outcome when he appeared at York Assizes court three months later charged with murder and on trial for his life. The judge, Mr Justice Atkin, certainly thought so, telling the jury before opening the case that he believed they would have no difficulty in returning a bill for murder.

Burkitt's counsel, Rowan Hamilton, played the only card the defence had. He submitted that Mrs Tyler had provoked his client through her continual nagging and suggested the attack was committed in a momentary fit of frenzy without any real intended malice. Summing up, the judge said mere nagging was not justification for violence and, in yet another obvious hint to the jury, warned it would be dangerous to reduce the charge to manslaughter simply because the defendant was nagged by the woman he lived with.

Nonetheless, the jury found him guilty of manslaughter rather than murder and Burkitt was sentenced to 12 years in prison. Winning the sympathy of a jury was to become something of a habit.

With remission for good behaviour, Burkitt actually served nine years in jail before being released in 1924 and was soon living off Hessle Road again earning his living as a fisherman. Unable to resist the charms of older women, he was also busy trying to woo 44-year-old Mrs Ellen Spencer.

Like Polly Tyler, she had long been separated from her husband and was living with another man — a trawler cook named Harry Sargeson — when Burkitt first began seeing her, helped by the fact that Sargeson was frequently away at sea.

Unfortunately for Mrs Spencer, the similarities did not end there. Within a year of his release from prison she would be dead from stab wounds to the neck inflicted by a pocket knife, her blood-soaked body covered by a coat. Burkitt had struck again.

Her body had been found slumped on a couch in a downstairs room by her shocked daughter, Mrs Matilda Walkington, who was on a visit to her mother's home in Leslie Avenue, off Subway Street. The blinds had been drawn despite it being midday and Mrs Walkington then found the back door was unusually tied shut with a piece of string. A neighbour helped her force the door and the police were called when her eyes fell on the sight of her mother's body.

PC Arthur Douthwaite smelled gas as soon as he entered the house. In the upstairs front bedroom he found Burkitt lying semi-conscious on the bed. The hollow threat of suicide after Polly Tyler's death had been much more real this time. The constable quickly opened a window and managed to revive the dazed man sufficiently enough to take him to an ambulance which had arrived at the scene.

What happened next on the journey to Hull Royal Infirmary and on arrival at the hospital was to prove the turning point in Burkitt's trial when he appeared in the now familiar surroundings of York Assizes court just over three weeks later.

Having recovered from his ordeal, he was charged with Mrs Spencer's murder and his own attempted suicide — still a criminal offence in those days.

With the law preventing his previous criminal record being made known to the jury, the prosecution relied heavily on an alleged confession made by Burkitt to PC Douthwaite in the ambulance. According to the police officer, Burkitt admitted stabbing Mrs Spencer on the couch with a pocket knife because he was "jealous of another man". On arrival at the infirmary, a statement was prepared verifying what he had said in the ambulance and was agreed by Burkitt in the presence of a doctor. Before being taken to a ward, he even revealed the knife was in a kitchen drawer.

A police search of the house duly found the knife where he had said it would be. Although there was no obvious sign of blood on it, an analyst later found tiny traces on the blade. In the kitchen were a pair of boots and a pair of trousers which Burkitt admitted were his. There was blood on both, with the trousers appearing to have been recently rubbed or washed.

The defence poured scorn on the suggested motive of jealousy. Apart from the alleged statement made in the ambulance, it was claimed there was no evidence to show Burkitt had been jealous of anyone. The jury, it was suggested, were being asked to make something of a statement made by a confused man en route to hospital.

This ignored earlier evidence from a doctor who had attended the house and briefly examined Burkitt before he left. The doctor thought he had almost completely recovered from inhaling the gas. Confused or not, Burkitt had also told the police exactly where to find the knife.

Doubts over the statement were re-inforced by Burkitt's own evidence from the witness box. He said he could not remember any statement being read over to him at the hospital. However, his memory of the events leading up to the death of Mrs Spencer was crystal clear.

He told the court he had turned up at her house after drinking seven pints of beer that night in a local pub. He was dozing off on the couch when he suddenly felt her put her hand in his pocket.

"I jumped up and threw the woman on the couch, after which I put my hands on the table but I did not know what I had got hold of. I lifted up my hand to frighten her and then I realised what I had in my hand," he said.

He claimed he never had any intention of killing her and denied being jealous. He was not angry with her at the time and put the tragedy down to the fact that he was too drunk to realise what he was doing. Drunkenness, suggested the defence, was a valid if exceptionable excuse for his behaviour. His version of the stabbing conflicted with the police finding no signs of a struggle in the house but even the judge, Sir Hugh Frazer, seemed swayed by his performance. In summing up, Sir Hugh said Burkitt had possibly been provoked by the woman and he added: "If the scales of justice are balanced evenly for and against the prisoner, then it is the duty of the judge to put into the balance a few grains of mercy".

The jury duly obliged and found him not guilty to murder but guilty to manslaughter. As Burkitt began a ten-year sentence, one wonders what the jury must have thought when the following day's newspapers revealed details of his previous almost identical killing. He was released from his second spell in prison for manslaughter in 1935 and, like before, returned to the Hessle Road community he knew so well, once more working as a fisherman.

One can only speculate what that same community thought of Billy Burkitt being back in its midst but by 1937 he was living with Mrs Emma Brookes in a tiny terrace off Neptune Street. She was four years younger than him but otherwise she mirrored Burkitt's previous ill-fated lovers, being married but separated from her husband. She was also known to drink quite heavily and was a sociable sort, much to the annoyance of her jealous lover.

Despite his own amorous advances in the past, Burkitt often accused her of seeing other men when he was at sea and frequently flew into jealous rages. As it turned out, for once he was probably right. On one occasion he followed Mrs Brookes and a trawlerhand, Thomas Fletcher, from a pub and surprised the couple by punching her in the back of the neck before shouting at her. Fletcher took off his coat and squared up for a fight but Burkitt ran off. Later Fletcher revealed he had been deceived into thinking Emma Brookes had been faithful only to him during the 18 months he had been seeing her when back in port. Infact, she seems to have divided her time between the two men.

Burkitt also complained that Emma would pawn his clothes to get money for drink and to spend on herself when he was away at sea. He told her sister-in-law he intended leaving her and added: "Look at me, I am in rags. She played with your brother for 25 years but she will not play with me. She will be a dead woman."

This threat — all the more chilling because of his past — was duly carried out on February 27 1939. The day before, Burkitt had returned home from sea and the couple were soon out drinking together in a nearby pub. Known to local children as Uncle Bill and Aunt Emma, they had arranged to take 14-year-old Peggy Chester to the cinema as a treat for the errands she often ran for Mrs Brookes. On the afternoon of the 27th, Peggy unknowingly became the last person to see Emma Brookes alive when she called and was told to come back after tea-time for her treat. Burkitt also asked her to bring back some aspirins and gave her an empty bottle to fill.

In between the girl calling, neighbours later said they heard sounds of quarrelling in the house and then saw Burkitt standing at the end of the terrace looking wild and distraught. He was heard to shout: "I am fed up with her. She is at it again," before disappearing back inside. When Peggy Chester called again, he answered the door and said the cinema trip was off because Mrs Brookes was asleep upstairs. The girl then froze as Burkitt switched the light off and lurched towards her, saying: "You daren't stay with me in the dark?". Terrified, she ran off but returned the next day only to find the door locked.

Burkitt was next seen on March 1 when he turned up at his sister Maria's home in Witty Street just after 7.30am. At first she thought he was drunk as he was frothing at the mouth and making little or no sense. Along with her husband she managed to lay him on a couch but her brother refused to say what was wrong until they were alone together. Then he blurted out: "I think I am dying. I have taken 600 aspirins." Either he had miscounted or his inability to commit suicide had been proven once again. No doubt fearing the worst, his sister asked about Emma but Burkitt just shrugged his shoulders and claimed he had caught her the day before with another man. Semi-recovered, he ran out of the house ignoring his sister's pleas that he should see a doctor. "Goodbye," he told her. "To tell you the truth I have killed her."

As the police were called out to Mrs Brookes' house, a railway policeman met Burkitt crossing Liverpool Street Bridge. The officer thought he looked dazed, noticed he was swaying about and asked him if he was feeling well. "Oh yes," replied Burkitt. "I only feel a bit groggy. Don't worry about me, I'll soon be all right." Five hours later Burkitt was being fished out of the Humber after yet another futile suicide attempt. He had been spotted by workmen clinging onto a wooden post off Sammy's Point, near to the mouth of the River Hull.

At Neptune Terrace, Emma Brookes' body was found lying on her bed, fully clothed except for her shoes which had been placed neatly on the floor. Bruises on both sides of her neck clearly showed she had been strangled and a bone in her neck was fractured. Once again, there were no signs of a struggle and death had almost certainly been instant. Next to the bed was a water jug containing diluted aspirin. Five empty 100-tablet

31

bottles of the pain-killer were found in a dustbin.

Burkitt appeared in court three days later after a spell in hospital recovering from his soaking in the river. Aged 53 and grey-haired and unshaven, he must have been a pathetic sight as he was still in the mud-splattered shabby navy blue suit he was wearing when rescued from the Humber.

Again charged with murder, his trial was this time held at Leeds Assizes court with the prosecution alleging jealousy as the motive. His threats against Mrs Brookes were detailed, as was his assault on her witnessed by Thomas Fletcher, the trawlerhand. The lack of any signs of a struggle in the bedroom was also highlighted. It appeared, suggested the prosecution, that Mrs Brookes was resting and had taken her shoes off for comfort. She might have even been asleep because there was nothing to show she had put up any form of resistance.

Burkitt entered the witness box and told how, despite living happily together for two years, Mrs Brookes had continued to see other men behind his back. He said he had even cut her housekeeping after discovering that she had pawned his clothes but denied ever making threats or arguing with her on the day she died.

He said she had gone to bed that afternoon after they both returned from a pub. He joined her and it was then she mentioned the names of two other men.

"When she said that it came as such a shock to me after my being so good to her, forgiving her, that everything seemed to go black," he told the hushed court.

"When I came round I found I had my hand on her throat. I could not believe it. I called her name, kissed her and shook her." Asked if he had any intention of killing her, he replied: "No, I loved her too much for that".

Shielded from Burkitt's previous record like their predecessors, the jury believed him, acquitted him of murder and found him guilty of manslaughter instead. Passing sentence, Mr Justice Cassels gave muted voice to his misgivings over the jury's verdict. Addressing Burkitt, he said: "The jury did not know what you and I knew — that this was the third time you have stood in the dock on a charge of murder.

"Each time it has been the murder of a woman with whom you have been living. Each time the jury have taken a merciful view. I can see in your case not one redeeming feature. You will be kept in penal servitude for the rest of your natural life."

Billy Burkitt's luck had run out but he was to remain Hull's most notorious serial killer for 40 years. In 1946 he appealed against his life sentence but three Appeal Court judges dismissed the challenge. However, Burkitt still managed to avoid spending the rest of his days behind bars. In early 1954 he was released on licence as he was suffering from incurable cancer and was admitted into hospital back in Hull. He died on Christmas Eve 1958 at the age of 69. A simple death notice in the Hull Daily Mail read; "You paid your debts dearly."

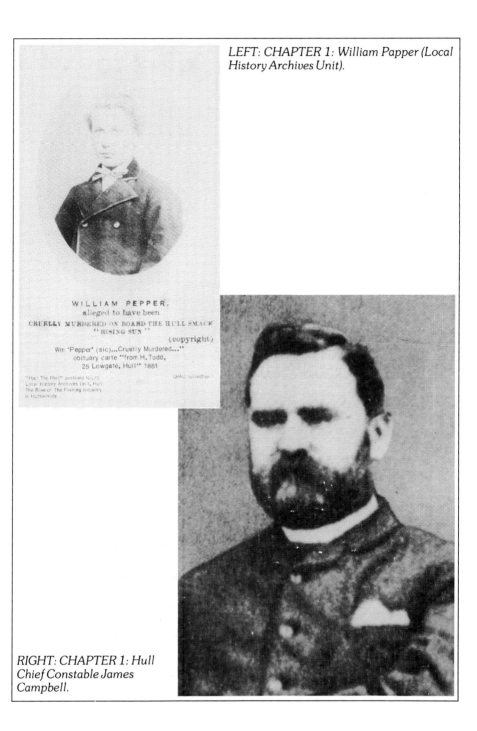

LEFT: CHAPTER 1: William Papper (Local History Archives Unit).

WILLIAM PEPPER,
alleged to have been
CRUELLY MURDERED ON BOARD THE HULL SMACK
"RISING SUN"
(copyright)
Wm 'Pepper' (sic)...Cruelly Murdered..."
obituary carte "'from H.Todd,
25 Lowgate, Hull'" 1881

"Past The Post" postcard No.15
Local History Archives Unit, Hull
The Rise of The Fishing Industry
in Humberside

LHAU collection

RIGHT: CHAPTER 1: Hull Chief Constable James Campbell.

LEFT: CHAPTER 1: The Rising Sun crew (Local History Archives Unit).

RIGHT: CHAPTER 1: Newspaper sketch of the assault on Papper.

Date	Name	Age	Vessel		Cause
,, 17	William Knapman -	20	John Brown -	,,	Taking in the jib and washed overboard by heavy sea.
November 27	George Houghton -	18	Bessie Lewis -	,,	Reefing the topsail and fell overboard.
,, 30	Thomas Chapman -	16	Alethia - -	,,	Washed overboard by heavy sea.
December 19	Henry Silby - -	18	Magic - -	,,	,, ,, ,,
,, ,,	Alfred Foster -	14	Speedwell -	,,	,, ,, ,,
,, ,,	George Holmes -	16	Sir Joseph -	,,	,, ,, ,,
1882. ✳ January 1	William Papper -	14	Rising Sun -	,,	Knocked overboard by the sail.
,, 6	Joseph Clinton -	20	William - -	,,	Washed overboard by heavy sea.
,, 7	August Fallengberg -	19	Olive-branch -	,,	Putting the top lift right and fell overboard.
,, 10	John W. Foster -	18	Albert - -	,,	Washed overboard by heavy sea.
,, ,,	George Cooper -	17	Winter - -	,,	,, ,, ,,
,, 19	George Camby -	17	Hope - --	,,	Drawing a bucket of water and fell overboard.
February 13	John Ridley -	20	Regulus -	Killed -	Struck by handle of winch, when heaving the gear, and killed.
,, 18	Richard Gorbeckett -	18	Loch Long -	Drowned	Reefing the sail and blown overboard.
,, 24	Peter Hoye -	16	Gleaner -	Drowned	Drawing a bucket of water and fell overboard.

ABOVE: CHAPTER 1: *Copy of Return of Fisherboys Drowned and Died at Sea, between Jan 1878 and Sept 1882.*

LEFT:CHAPTER 2: *Hull Jail circa 1780.*

RIGHT: CHAPTER 2: *Sketch of Arthur Richardson.*

LEFT:
CHAPTER 2:
York Prison (C.
Haines).

BELOW:
CHAPTER 2:
Hull Prison.

BELOW: CHAPTER 3: Mrs Emma
Brooks

NO. 105: NEW SERIES OF "MAIL" CARTOONS.

(SPECIALLY DRAWN FOR US BY MR M. J. MATTHEWS)

RIGHT:
CHAPTER 3:
Billy Burkitt
(True
Detective
Magazine.)

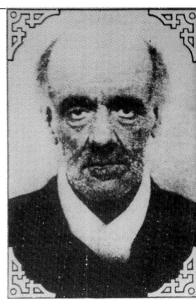

LEFT:
CHAPTER 4:
Dearnley's
Ray of Hope.

BELOW: CHAPTER 4: Tom Houghton.

A midnight telegram came . . . 'Your son is sentenced to death'

'I'LL NEVER BELIEVE TOM DID IT IN COLD BLOOD!'

SYMPATHY FOR A MOTHER

MOTHER WHO WILL NOT GIVE UP HOPE

SOMEWHERE under the burning desert sun in the Suez Canal zone, in a prison cell, lies a young Hull soldier condemned to death. Twenty-three-year-old Cpl. Tom Houghton, found guilty of killing an officer, waits in a small white-washed cell with iron bars at the window while the sentence passed on him at a court-martial last week, is reviewed.

For company in his cell the ground sheet. But thousands of miles away, in Hull, every Hull there is one person whose hopes are with him day and night.

and, like all mothers, now stoutly refuses to give up hope.

MOTHER'S FAITH

"When he wrote to me about the trial it was an awful shock. But he told me not to worry. Said he had a good lawyer and that everything would be all right.'

And a mother's faith shone out of her eyes

...... By ......
Marjorie
Stephenson

as she looked at her family gathered round her and whispered, 'I believe him; I think all will be well in the end. I shall yet see my boy again.'

LEFT: CHAPTER 4: Albert Pierrepoint (Press Association)

BELOW LEFT: CHAPTER 4: James Inglis under escort (Donald Innes).

BELOW: CHAPTER 5: Averyl Botterill.

ABOVE: CHAPTER 5:
Gladys Tate.

BELOW: CHAPTER 6:
Hull Royal Infirmary,
circa 1952.

RIGHT: CHAPTER 7:
Graham Stevenson on his
wedding day.

THE DAILY

No. 26,789   Telephone 27111 (21 lines)   HULL, THURSDAY, DECEMB

Hull wedding eve killer given a life sentence

Harold Needler lashes the F.A.

BRIAN TAYLOR

A 21-YEAR-OLD HULL LABOURER was sentenced to life imprisonment at Leeds Assizes this afternoon after being found guilty of the murder of a 16-year-old girl at his home only hours before his wedding.

After a 2½-hour retirement, the jury returned a majority verdict of 11 to 1 against Thomas Graham Stevenson, of 800, Hessle High-road, who pleaded not guilty to strangling Margaret Lucy Wainfer, whose body was found on Friday, August 13 in the back garden of 54, Woodcock-street, Hull, next door to the house he was preparing for his bride.

The verdict came only minutes after the jury had failed to reach a unanimous verdict, and were sent back by Mr Justice Hinchcliffe to try and reach a majority verdict.

Majority verdict

Revival bid

Tied tightly

Only hours earlier, a girl had died

A HAPPY wedding day. Only hours before that, the

HULL TRAGEDY.

MR FORSEY.

ABOVE: CHAPTER 7:
Sketch of Harry Forsey.

BELOW: CHAPTER 7:
Margaret Wainfer.

RIGHT: CHAPTER 8:
Humber Street, circa
1961.

THE KHAKI KILLERS

✝

I f Burkitt's various escapes from the death sentence were remarkable, Albert Dearnley's brush with the gallows was positively astonishing. No Hollywood scriptwriter could surely have come up with such an eleventh hour reprieve which left his family, friends and most of Hull simultaneously delighted and deeply puzzled. A Lance Corporal with the 1st Leicestershire Regiment, he was only 19-years-old when he stood trial in November 1923 accused of murdering his best friend, regimental drummer boy James Ellis. They had grown up together, living on opposite sides of the same tiny terrace of Nornabell Street, Holderness Road, before enlisting with the same regiment.

Ellis had gone missing from the regiment's Aldershot barracks in May that year and it was generally assumed he had deserted. Four months later his remains were found in woodland on the outskirts of the town. His arms and legs were tied together by a piece of drum rope, his head was covered with an Army overcoat and a gag had been stuffed into his mouth. Suffocation was regarded as the likely cause of death.

Albert Dearnley was quickly arrested but the teenager maintained his best friend's death had been a terrible accident. He claimed they had been planning to desert from the Army with America being their goal. On the day of Ellis' disappearance, he said they had gone for a drink and then for a walk. In drunken horseplay, Dearnley said a bizarre game of Cowboys and Indians developed in which he lassoed his friend with a length of rope. Ellis then asked to be bound and gagged, boasting he could still break free and beat Dearnley back to the camp. Ellis never re-appeared but Dearnley said he thought his friend had decided to desert on his own.

He changed his story slightly when he appeared before a jury at Hampshire Assizes court charged with his friend's murder. Although still claiming Ellis had asked to be tied up, he now said he bound him tightly as a punishment for insulting his girlfriend. Furthermore, he said he told Ellis he would return to free him the following day but never did because of his duties at the barracks.

The story failed to impress the jury and he was found guilty of murder and sentenced to death by execution on December 18.

The outcome of what had already been a closely-watched case in Hull caused an outcry in his home city. An appeal against the sentence was lodged on the grounds of mental instability, as three immediate members of his family were in mental asylums. Many felt the boy's father should have been called to give evidence and the Dearnley family's local vicar, the Rev E.A. Berry, began collecting a petition calling for his life to be spared. It eventually contained 32,000 signatures when it landed on the desk of the Home Secretary, Lord Bridgeman.

The pleas for mercy went unheeded but at least they caused a delay and allowed Dearnley to celebrate Christmas that year, albeit in a cell in Winchester Jail. The appeal against sentence was dismissed early in the New Year and a new date for his execution was fixed for Tuesday January 8 at 9am.

His father and stepmother saw him on the Monday morning after making the long train journey to Winchester. Prison rules dictated they should spend just 15 minutes together, with a warder sat either side of Dearnley who was himself sat ten feet away from his parents. They were not allowed to touch him but the few words that passed between them probably saved his life. Dearnley's father had been convinced his son had not acted alone and used this last meeting as a chance to test his theory that the boy was holding something back out of loyalty.

Asked if someone else was involved, Dearnley blurted out: "If anyone says Hilda Storey was in it, you can tell them that it is not true," before falling silent again. Hilda was his girlfriend but his father sensed there was more to tell. Whatever it was, they left the prison later that morning firmly believing they would never see him again. A grave for Dearnley had already been dug in a nearby cemetery and the hangman had sized him up for the necessary drop the next morning.

As his parents sadly embarked on the journey home, one of the most dramatic turnabouts ever heard of in a British murder case was beginning to unfold.

A last letter written by Dearnley to his sweetheart Hilda had been routinely intercepted by the prison authorities for censorship. In it, he said he had lied at the trial because the real truth would have brought shame on himself and his family. Aware of the concerns of the boy's father, the prison governor went to see Dearnley himself, dismissing the two warders from the cell. Only then did the true story emerge and within minutes the governor was on the telephone to the Home Office.

Dearnley's parents arrived back in Hull early in the evening bracing themselves for the grim task of passing on their son's last messages to the family. They went straight to the boy's grandparents' home in St Mark's Street but instead of finding grieving relations the house was full of celebration — the boy's execution had been postponed.

Mr Dearnley was stunned but delighted by the news saying it re-affirmed his suspicions. A regular attender at the local Salvation Army hall, he quickly visited Rev Berry, who was planning to open his church the next morning for prayer to coincide with the execution. Both men said the power of prayer had helped save the teenager, Mrs Dearnley recalled a black cat had crossed her path earlier that day.

But instead of clarifying the matter, the official statement from the Home Office announcing the postponement only caused further confusion. It simply said the Home Secretary had received "fresh information" from Dearnley himself concerning the murder and went on to say this was now to be "fully considered", prompting the postponement.

This "fresh information" was a mystery to his parents, who repeatedly went over what they thought at the time was their last meeting with him, trying to remember some hint in the conversation which could provide a clue.

Speculation in the Press intensified when it was revealed that soldiers from Dearnley's battalion had been ordered to attend the War Office in London in connection with the case. A reporter visiting the Dearnley household in Alpha Terrace two days later found the boy's father nailing a photograph of his son to the wall, surrounded by flags and a regimental scroll. The picture was next to a large coloured portrait of General William Booth, founder of the Salvation Army.

Despite the postponement, Dearnley's fate was far from certain. Reports from Winchester suggested that even if he had implicated another in the murder he would still hang.

Then on January 10, newspapers reported that a Sergeant H. Ormes of the 1st Leicesters, had been among the soldiers to be called first to the War Office and then the Home Office for a series of interviews.

Ormes belonged to the same company as the two teenagers and had given evidence at Dearnley's trial. A married man with two children, his Army career spanned 14 years, serving in India and in France during the First World War.

At Aldershot, Dearnley had acted as his batman, or servant, a not uncommon role among the lower ranks. Ormes' sister-in-law was Hilda Storey and her photograph in the sergeant's married quarters quickly captured the heart of the young lance corporal from Hull. When the pretty dressmaker from Bishop Auckland visited Aldershot, a romance began and the couple soon became engaged.

During his trial, Dearnley said Ellis had been jealous of his relationship with Hilda and had insulted her at a dance in the barracks. Hilda also gave evidence in court, dramatically dressed in all black and bursting into tears as she entered the witness box for the first time.

Now that her fiancee's execution had been postponed, she recalled the first and only time she had met Ellis. "He seemed to me silly and very jealous," she told reporters still anxious to find an explanation for the dramatic events.

Dearnley's bewildered parents were thrown into further confusion with the arrival of a letter from their son, written earlier in the week before the postponement was announced. The words were those of a man convinced he was about to die, with again no hint of the belated "fresh information" which was to follow.

On Friday January 11, the Home Office confirmed the news his family had prayed for in a brief announcement which yet again left questions unanswered. It read: "The investigation of the further information furnished by the prisoner Dearnley has now been completed. While the result does not touch the validity of the verdict of the jury, the Home Secretary has come to the conclusion that it affords ground for the remission of the death sentence, and he has accordingly advised the King to commute the sentence to one of penal servitude for life".

The mysterious additional evidence given by Dearnley remained locked away in a secret Home Office file for over 70 years until it was recently published for the first time. Dearnley himself was sworn to secrecy and at the time of his reprieve was quoted as saying simply that his conscience had now been cleared.

The truth was that Sgt Ormes had seduced the young lance corporal and the pair were having a secret homosexual affair when Ellis walked in one day and caught them in the act. Inflamed with jealousy, Ellis demanded that Dearnley become his lover, too, and threatened to expose his old friend and the sergeant to the authorities if he refused.

When Dearnley began his relationship with Hilda, Ellis became even more jealous and issued yet more blackmail threats until Dearnley's temper finally snapped and he ended up killing him.

Homosexual activity was still a serious criminal offence but its factor in the case convinced Home Office officials that, as additional evidence, it could have been enough to persuade the jury to opt for a verdict of manslaughter. Confirmation came from Ormes who, because of the exceptional circumstances, was told he would be spared from prosecution if he told the truth, even if it did incriminate him.

The sergeant knew his Army career was over but his subsequent confession did help create an unlikely piece of military history.

Twenty eight years later, another East Hull household was gripped with the same uncertainty that a death sentence always brought.

Tom Houghton, a 23-year-old soldier, had been serving with the Royal Army Supply Corps in the Suez Canal zone as tension between Britain and Egypt increased in early 1952.

Thoughts of conflict were, however, temporarily banished one Saturday night in February that year when the canteen of Houghton's unit was transformed into a makeshift birthday party venue and music and laughter filled the air.

A single man, Houghton had been in the Canal zone for three years and was keenly pursuing a 20-year-old Greek girl, Iro Hadjifoti, who worked as a typist at the camp.

He had already written to his sister Stella back in England telling her that he was courting a Greek girl and thinking of marrying her. In fact, Houghton's relationship with the typist was nothing more than a romantic fantasy on his part. The had never gone out together and his unwanted attention got so bad that the day before the party he had been ordered to stay away from the girl either on or off duty.

Houghton had little time for Captain Herbert Mason, who had issued the order, and on the night of the party he peered through the canteen window and saw Mason dancing with 'his' Iro.

The furious corporal stormed back to his tent, seized a machine gun and began loading the weapon. A private tried to pull him back but Houghton threatened to shoot him before opening fire and hitting another corporal who had attempted to grab the gun off him.

Marching out towards the canteen Houghton fired off a number of single shots, hitting another soldier in the arm before Capt Mason and a sergeant emerged from the canteen to investigate the sound of gunfire. They met Houghton holding the weapon on the canteen verandah. As the sergeant made a dive for Houghton's feet, Mason ordered him to hand over the gun. Houghton dodged clear and opened fire at Mason from point-blank range.

The captain collapsed in a pool of blood as Houghton turned the gun on another soldier, shooting him in the foot and back before pouring a burst of gunfire through the canteen doorway. More shots were fired at Mason as he lay wounded before a sergeant inside the canteen fired at Houghton with a pistol, hitting him in the foot and knocking him over.

Mason died in hospital from seven separate bullet wounds. Although he had been drinking and had earlier thrown a beer bottle against a wall, witnesses agreed that Houghton had not been drunk.

At the court-martial in Fayid, Iro Hadjifoti — exotically referred to as "the girl in blue" throughout the proceedings — denied his claims that she had promised to marry him and even the defence counsel conceded Houghton had delusions about their supposed relationship.

The defence asked for a verdict of guilty but insane, claiming he was "a decent man, a friend to his friends, who had suddenly turned into a raving lunatic" because of mad jealousy. But the judge-advocate, Mr F.H. Dean. ignored the defence pleas and on finding him guilty duly sentenced Houghton to death by hanging.

As he languished in his cell in a military prison, attention turned to Stirling Terrace in Hull where his small, grey-haired mother, Elizabeth, lived. A widow, she received confirmation of her son's fate in a telegram from the War Office and immediately wrote to the Queen pleading for a Royal reprieve.

A petition was also launched, signed first by the Lord Mayor and eventually by 40,000 others in the city and from around the country. The East Hull MP, Commander Harry

Pursey, presented the petition in person to the War Office but to no avail. Subsequent appeal hearings upheld the death sentence and a British Embassy spokesman in Cairo announced the petition had failed as Mrs Houghton arrived by train in London en route to Egypt for a last emotional meeting with her son.

Unlike the Dearnley family before her, there was no unexpected twist of fate after her specially arranged 24-hour visit to Fayid, which was her first trip abroad. Mrs Houghton had not seen her son for two years but the Army authorities conceded to her request that his body be buried in consecrated ground in a nearby British military cemetery, an honour not normally afforded to convicted criminals.

The last act in the drama was carried out on June 24 by the executioner Albert Pierrepoint, arguably the most famous British hangman this century.

Pierrepoint's father, Henry, and uncle Tom were both hangmen before him. As teenagers the Pierrepoint brothers lived in Hull with their parents in Chalk Lane, off Hessle Road, with the menfolk of the family working on the construction of Alexandra Dock.

Henry Pierrepoint resigned as a hangman in 1914 but young Albert undoubtedly took inspiration from his uncle Tom, who sucked sweets during executions and once advised his nephew: "If you can't do without whisky, don't do it at all".

Tom Pierrepoint was obsessively secret about his work but gave a rare interview while carrying out the last ever execution in Hull in April 1936, when he hanged Lincolnshire woman Ethel Major who had poisoned her husband. In the interview, he happily recalled his childhood days in Hull, from selling vegetables to visiting the Rising Sun fishing smack after the sensational arrest of its skipper Otto Brand for the murder cf young William Papper.

Albert Pierrepoint went on to record 400 executions in his career, around half being Nazi war criminals, including Lord "Haw Haw' Joyce, who carried out propaganda radio broadcasts for the Germans, and the notorious Belsen concentration camp commander Joseph Kramer. Once, he managed to hang 27 Nazis in just one day.

At the time of Houghton's execution in 1952, a Royal Commission was wrestling over whether capital punishment for murder should be limited or modified. The Commission had been asked to review the method of carrying out the death penalty, rather than whether it should be abolished.

Published a year later, its main recommendations included delegating Pierrepoint's responsibilities to allow for the availability of other 'qualified' executioners. In effect, his monopoly was over.

In July 1955, Ruth Ellis became the last woman to be hanged in Britain and Albert Pierrepoint was her executioner. Seven months later he resigned after nearly 24 years of hanging. It has been claimed the Ellis case affected him so badly that it forced his hand but in his autobiography he suggests his retirement was hastened by a dispute with the Home Office over expenses. His book also dismisses the notion that the death penalty acted as a deterrent.

"I have come to the conclusions that executions solve nothing, and are only an antiquated relic of a primitive desire for revenge which takes the easy way and hands over the responsibility of revenge to other people," he wrote.

"All the men and women whom I have faced at the final moment convince me that in what I have done I have not prevented a single murder."

A case in point was that of James Inglis who was executed by Pierrepoint in 1951. The lack of any petition for a reprieve probably underlined the public's distaste over the murder of 50-year-old divorcee and prostitute Alice Morgan, who was found dead in her Eton Terrace home in Hull, beaten and strangled with one of her own stockings.

The 28-year-old's defence rested on a claim of insanity at the resulting trial but a prison doctor virtually sealed his fate by declaring him mentally fit. Drink and an argument over how much he was prepared to pay for Mrs Morgan's services were the more plausible reasons put forward for his crime. When the Leeds Assizes jury returned a guilty verdict, the judge Mr Justice Corman asked Inglis if he had anything to say before the death sentence was announced. "I have had a fair trial," came the reply from the dock. "All I ask now is that you get me hanged as soon as possible."

Eager to help his executioner, Inglis famously ran to the gallows from his condemned cell, ensuring his hanging was over from start to finish in just seven seconds.

The last hanging in England took place in August 1964. Five years later, the death penalty for murder was finally abolished.

UNFIT TO PLEAD

✝

I n cases of murder, the climax of an investigation into the crime usually comes in court. A not guilty plea by the defendant will ensure the thrust and parry of prosecution and defence counsel, evidence from witnesses and the accused, and a final decision by the jury. An early admission of guilt is more rare but can, by its very nature, be just as dramatic. Straightforward or complex, murder trials rarely fail to capture and fire the public's interest and imagination. Yet one outcome remains as tantalizingly puzzling to the public as the reason for the crime being committed in the first place.

Deciding if a defendant is unfit to plead is technically a task for a jury if the issue is raised by either prosecution or defence before a trial can begin, although a judge will usually direct a jury on its decision after hearing evidence. Deciding if a defendant is capable of pleading depends on expert medical evidence and often centres on whether that person understands what they have been charged with or is able to comprehend the proceedings of a criminal trial, including the ability to give evidence and properly instruct their own counsel.

Unlocking the mind of a killer can be a torturous business but in the closed world of the mentally-ill and the certifiably insane, the act of murder remains a maddening mystery which can stay unexplained forever, as was the case in two of the area's most shocking murder inquiries of this century.

In October 1934 Walter Smith was working as a labourer at the Hull Fish Meal and Oil

Works on St Andrew's Dock. He was on a night shift taking a break to eat his supper when he noticed a light coming towards him from the direction of Hessle. It was two o'clock in the morning and the last thing he was expecting to see was a cyclist approaching from such a remote spot to the west of the dock. As the figure drew nearer, Smith's surprise turned to shock when he realised that as well as the man on the bike there was a naked child propped up on the handlebars.

Smith ran towards the cyclist, still not sure of what he was seeing in the gloom of the night. The breathless cyclist stopped his machine and blurted out: "It's a youngster I've found in a pond up yonder. He is only four-years-old and we've been looking for him since eight o'clock."

The cyclist, who Smith would later say looked nervous, dismounted and asked him to hold the cycle while he covered the child up. After taking off his overcoat and dropping it over the tiny child's body, the cyclist was asked where he was going now. "I want to get him home as sharp as I can," came the reply, but instead Smith suggested the police box at the lock-head of the dock. To his relief, the cyclist took his advice and rode off, heading for the lock-head without another word. Smith could not be sure because of the pitch dark but he thought he had seen blood on the child's body.

Fred Fuller had searched enthusiastically for little Kenneth Staff after the youngster had been reported missing from his home in Picturesque Terrace, Manchester Street, at 8pm the previous evening. A month away from his fifth birthday, he was one of three children; the youngest, a sister, having been born a week earlier.

In the maze of streets and terraces off Hessle Road, everyone knew everyone else and Fuller, a 20-year-old unemployed labourer, was a familiar sight to all, usually to be spotted on his beloved bike. He lived in Manchester Street with his mother who had been friends with Kenny Staff's mother for some years. After the boy's father had reported him missing to the police and began a search of his own, Fuller called next door where Mrs Staff's sister lived and offered to help look for the boy. He returned twice more to ask if Kenny had been found before going to a friend's house for supper.

It was now 10.30pm and Jack Kitchen, who lived in another terrace off Manchester Street, suggested a fresh search for the boy as he and Fuller finished their meal. Kitchen also knew Kenny and soon they were heading for Gordon Street police station to find out if the youngster had been found. When they reached the station, Fuller refused to go inside so Kitchen spoke to a policeman who said the child was still missing. Fuller, who had been wearing a jacket, trousers and flat cap, then walked home for his bicycle and an overcoat before returning to his friend's home. Kitchen again suggested searching together but Fuller said: "It will upset you. I will find him if it takes me while the morning."

Nellie Wallace, another neighbour of Fuller, saw him pass by her house at 11.30pm and he spoke of the missing child. She thought Kenny might have fallen asleep in a back alley and said Fuller should start looking there. "Oh, he won't be down there," came the reply. Unknown to both Kitchen and Wallace, not to mention Kenny's worried aunt living next door, Fred Fuller already knew exactly where the boy was.

Also unknown to those who he talked with after 8pm was the fact that Fuller had been the last person to be seen with the youngster some two hours earlier.

A schoolboy, Raymond West, had seen Fuller ask Kenny if he wanted an apple as the boy ran along Manchester Street just as it was turning dark. Kenny was then lifted on the bike's handlebars before Fuller rode off. Fish worker Jane Barnes even asked Fuller what he was doing, pointing out that he was risking a £5 fine by carrying a passenger on his handlebars. "That's nothing; I would go 'up the road' for that but where I'm going they won't see me," he told her.

A railwayman in charge of a crossing on St Andrew's dock was the next person to see Fuller and the boy perched on the front of the bike as they stopped for a passing train. Then it was the turn of Percy Jordan, who was fishing on the dock foreshore. He recognised Fuller as the youth rode past with the child. About an hour later, at around 7.30pm, Fuller returned from the direction of Hessle alone. Jordan asked him for a match and the youth obliged after getting off his cycle. "He seemed to be in an agitated state and was blinking as though he needed spectacles," Jordan would recall later.

PC Thomas Cawkill was on duty at the police box near what was known as the Billingsgate railway crossing on St Andrew's dock when he saw the cyclist approach from the direction of the Fish Meal Company. It was now 2.10am and the two constables from the East Riding force who huddled in the police box could hardly believe their eyes. Fuller told the startled officers: "I found this body floating about in a pond on the Humber foreshore near the railway lines". As a PC Harkness telephoned for the city police, Fuller carried the body into the police box while PC Cawkill asked the cyclist if he knew the boy. To his surprise, Fuller gave Kenneth Staff's full name and address.

A brief statement given in the police box by Fuller was repeated to detectives as he led a small party on foot to the spot where he said he had found the boy. Included in the party was the East Riding police surgeon, Dr H. E. Watts-Waters, and the men carried torches to pick their way through the gloom. Fuller said he had last seen Kenny Staff just before 8pm and had given him an apple but claimed the boy had run off after going to his friend Jack Kitchen's home to change a penny. As he ended his account of finding the body in the pond, Fuller concluded: "He has been 'ticed him away because he could not walk all that way on his own. Somebody has given him some goodies."

Even cloaked in darkness, the pond was indeed remote. Although known locally as a fish pond it was actually a disused brick pit between the railway line and the River Humber just beyond the city boundary line. It was the best part of two miles from Kenny Staff's home. With Fuller pointing to the spot where he said he had found the body, police officers shone their torches across a deep dry ditch and into the pond. About 12 feet away the torchlight picked out a grey-coloured object floating on the surface. Fuller cried out: "That's his shirt, that's the boy's shirt!"

He was taken to Hessle police station while detectives began to piece together Kenny Staff's last known movements. They soon realised they dovetailed perfectly with

Fuller's. At first light officers returned to the pond and duly recovered most of the boy's clothing as witnesses were tracked down. Several later picked out Fuller in an identity parade as the cyclist last seen giving a ride to the boy.

After initially denying that he had caused the boy's death, Fuller eventually offered to give a statement admitting his guilt. In it, he spoke of taking Kenny to the pond and attacking him with a pair of scissors. As the youngster started to scream he pushed him into the pond, punched him in the face and left him. Returning to the scene at 2am and finding the boy was drowned, he pulled him out, took his clothes off and threw them back into the water before wrapping the body in his coat and placing it on his bike.

The post-mortem concluded death was caused by asphyxia due to drowning and shock. The boy had suffered a single stab wound to the body and extensive bruising to the head and face. Dr Watts-Waters said considerable force had been used to inflict the injuries and found the wound was likely to have been caused by scissors. A blood-stained pair of scissors were later found in Fuller's house together with a bloodied pair of trousers which he had changed on the night of the boy's disappearance after returning from the Gordon Street police station to fetch his bike, supposedly to continue the search.

Charged with the boy's murder, Fuller then attempted to change his confession, claiming instead that another man who he could not name had grabbed the toddler on the foreshore and killed him. He even claimed the mystery man lived in Scarborough Street and offered to lead the police to his house but in reality it appeared to be a last clumsy bid to clear his name. Nobody took this belated statement seriously but in the month before his trial at York Assizes, Fuller's sanity became a very serious topic for debate.

He spent his remand at Armley Jail in Leeds where the prison doctor twice visited him in his cell. The doctor also consulted with two medical officers at the jail who had regular contact with Fuller while in custody there. His report on Fuller's mental condition effectively ended the trial before it even began.

The doctor concluded that Fuller was quite incapable of understanding his offence or the penalties that went with it. He was satisfied the youth was insane, both now and at the time of the killing. Today, the question of the defendant's mental stability when considering the ability to enter a plea is the subject of far greater medical evidence and scrutiny but this was 1934 and, using the terminology of the day, trial judge Mr Justice Porter said the evidence was clear that Fuller was "a lunatic when he committed the offence and a lunatic now".

The proceedings lasted only a few minutes as the jury duly found him insane and unfit to plead. He was sent back to jail to await a permanent place in a mental hospital.

Nearly 30 years later, Victor Wilson stood in the same York Assizes court as Fuller had done in a brief hearing destined to have the same outcome. The similarities between the two were uncanny; Wilson had also been medically examined while on remand at Armley, it was also agreed he could not hope to comprehend the proceedings and it was agreed he had little idea of the seriousness of the offences which, like Fuller's, had been committed just outside Hull's city boundary.

But the similarities did not end there. The killing of a child invariably provokes public incomprehension and the same feeling was evident as the gruesome facts in Wilson's case emerged, although he was charged with the double murder of two farmers' wives. Gladys Tate and Averyl Botterill were neighbours in the tiny hamlet of Meaux, which lies between Wawne and Routh. In the early 1960s the countryside around Meaux still belonged to another world away from the expanding city of Hull where planners were drawing up proposals for the huge council estate of Bransholme to be built to the south of Wawne village itself.

Although there was an age gap of over 30 years between them, the two women were firm friends. Gladys Tate was 53-years old and lived with her husband, Albert, at the foreman's house at Abbey Farm in Meaux. Married for 10 years, her husband worked on the farm and had three grown-up children from a previous marriage. The Tates had lived at the farm for six years and were able to offer a welcome to a pair of newly-weds when they moved into a nearby cottage. Unable to find a house in Leconfield where he worked on a farm, Kenneth Botterill and his wife, Averyl, settled in a vacant cottage in Meaux. He remained working in Leconfield, travelling each day by motorcycle, while she found a job in a small pottery in nearby Routh. The two women soon became friends, visiting each other for tea, and they began taking regular Sunday afternoon walks together in the countryside while their husbands worked.

Sunday, September 8 1963, was seemingly no different from countless others they had spent together. Averyl Botterill cycled to her neighbour's house and they set off to pick wild blackberries accompanied, as ever, by Gladys Tate's faithful dog.

But it was not an ordinary Sunday for Eric Ribey and his wife, who lived at a nearby farmhouse. In the last two months their home had been entered at least six times, the most recent being the previous evening when they had returned to find a light shining through a door they knew had been closed. The break-ins all followed a similar disturbing pattern for the only things stolen were items of Mrs Ribey's clothing. In addition, zip fasteners had been broken, buttons pulled from coats and the high heels on a pair of shoes had been mysteriously cracked. The police investigated the incidents and agreed to post a special watch on the house that Sunday night.

Averyl Botterill also had cause to worry while the Ribeys became more concerned about the bizarre burglaries and changed their door locks. The 20-year-old was aware that she was now being regularly followed and spied on by a man as she went about her business.

That Sunday afternoon, Eric Ribey's wife refused to go upstairs alone to make the bed — so great was her terror of what she might find. Her husband went up with her, carrying a pair of binoculars to look out of the window across the surrounding countryside just in case he spotted anything unusual. Within minutes his gaze fell upon the figure of a man crossing a gap in a hedge near the farm buildings some 300 yards away. The man's movements were hurried and seconds later the sound of a gun being fired rocked Eric Ribey back on his heels. The man appeared again in the distance, this time partially hidden behind a wall, stooping down and then standing up straight again. By now, Eric Ribey was on the phone to the police.

PC John Pepys was patrolling in the area and was soon looking through Mr Ribey's binoculars to the spot where the man had been seen. Cautiously, he left the Ribeys' farmhouse and approached the scene walking in an arc, noticing a slight stain of blood on a car track. Going through a gate into a field, he was only a few feet away from the man who had aroused Eric Ribey's suspicions. Horrified by what he saw, PC Pepys immediately knew the worried farmer had been right to call. The man stood with his back to him, wiping his brow with one arm and apparently touching the bottom part of his stomach with his other. Beyond the man lay the naked body of Averyl Botterill, lying on the ground surrounded by her clothes which had been ripped and torn. Beside them was a double-barrelled shotgun and a blood-covered sheath knife stuck fast into the ground.

The constable challenged the man, who simply said: "One thing led to another and that was it". As he arrested and cautioned the man, PC Pepys noticed marks on the dead woman's neck and a nearby discarded nylon stocking. Swaying by his side, the man staggered forward and nearly fell over. "I understand," he replied to the caution, "I have always wanted to dress up in women's clothes".

Eric Ribey immediately recognised the man with PC Pepys when they both came back into his view. It was Bruce Wilson, a 20-year-old farmhand who lived in the same cluster of cottages as the Botterills. The Ribeys knew Wilson well as he had gone to the same school as their son and had occasionally shared a meal with them. A quiet youth who lived with his grandparents, Wilson had no girlfriend and his only young female company was when Averyl Botterill called in most nights after work for a cup of tea with his grandmother. He would also sometimes go out shooting with the Botterills and Albert Tate, carrying his prized shotgun which he had saved so hard to buy.

Wilson was the man Mrs Botterill believed was tracking her. She had been told by her husband to ignore him but now those fears had been terribly realised.

Back at his patrol car, PC Pepys asked Wilson if he knew the dead woman they had just left lying in the field. He not only named her but stunned the officer by saying: "There's another one as well, you know, in the wood by the path". Wilson told how he had shot Gladys Tate and, after strangling her young friend, had dragged her body into a nearby wood.

Mrs Tate's body was quickly found with gunshot wounds to the head. Her dog was discovered nearby, killed by the second cartridge from Wilson's shotgun. The young farmhand was taken to Beverley's police station where he made a statement, recounting his love of wearing women's clothing since being a young teenager, the recent break-ins he had carried out in the area and the way he had stalked the two women before hiding in a bush and cold-bloodedly shooting Mrs Tate as they approached. It ended with perhaps Wilson's most sickening confession, one which police officers at the scene had hoped was not true. After strangling Mrs Botterill, Wilson had first dragged Mrs Tate's body into the wood before returning to violate the body of his younger victim.

Even more unsettling for the detectives now quizzing him was Wilson's apparent lack of concern over the charges he was facing. A keen motor racing fan, one of the first questions he asked after being taken into custody was whether the famous British driver Jim Clarke had won an important televised race that afternoon.

In Wilson's room, police found exercise books filled with stories written in pencil about motor racing. Alongside them were lurid sexual fantasies penned by Wilson, together with a bundle of pin-up magazines in a cardboard box. Under the bed was a pile of women's clothes, ranging from underwear to a green dress belonging to Mrs Ribey which had been stolen the night before. Most chilling of all was one sketch of women being gagged and violently stripped naked and another of a man and a woman above the words: 'Decree nisa (sic), final and absolute. Granted 13th September, 1963, to Timothy Botterill on the grounds of adultery by Joan Averyl Botterill with unown (sic) man'.

Wilson continued to show little understanding, let alone remorse over his crimes while in Armley Prison awaiting a trial which would never take place. The prison's senior medical officer, Dr George Wray, would later tell trial judge Mr Justice McNair that Wilson's reaction to the charges during his remand was almost non-existent. "It is something I can only say is of light-hearted unconcern," he explained. Both Dr Wray and Dr James Valentine, a consultant psychiatrist and lecturer at Leeds University, formed the same opinion — in their view Wilson was suffering from schizophrenia. Dr Valentine suggested he did not know he had done any sort of wrong. The jury took a matter of seconds to decide Wilson was unfit to plead. After a hearing that lasted only 25 minutes, Mr Justice McNair said: "I am perfectly satisfied it is of great importance he should be kept in a place of safety so that there is no possibility of his being at large".

DIAMOND JIM
AND THE
BLUEBIRD STABBING

✝

O ne of the last Hull murder cases in which the death sentence was passed was another featuring military personnel. But instead of the familiar sight of British uniforms on display, the dock was filled with four men wearing the blue of the United States Air Force and carrying their distinctive peaked caps by their sides. It was May 1956 and four American airmen from the USAF base at Holme on Spalding Moor stood accused of murdering 27-year-old Walter Beaumont in a late-night brawl in a dockside Hull cafe.

The fact that all four were black was deemed newsworthy enough to mention prominently in newspaper reports of the day, sharing space devoted to coverage of the American's latest hydrogen bomb tests in the Pacific. The novelty of the men's colour and their role, albeit small, in the developing drama of the Cold War undoubtedly helped pack the public benches when they made their first appearances before the city's magistrates.

The plasterer's labourer had been stabbed in the stomach and died a week later in hospital. He had been drinking with a friend in the Bluebird cafe in Mytongate, which was also known as Jama's, the nickname of the proprietor.

Now demolished along with the street where it once stood, the Bluebird was a late-night haunt serving up after-hours drinks. Frequented mainly by seamen, prostitutes and anyone with sufficient amounts of Dutch courage to enter through the front door, it was also something of a magnet for the off-duty American airmen from Holme on Spalding Moor who regularly visited Hull's dance halls on their free evenings. Beaumont had been with Ernest Milns, a flour miller, and it was Milns who first tangled with the Americans in the cafe, although the reason for the brawl starting was never satisfactorily explained at the men's trial.

Some witnesses said the airmen began taunting the cafe proprietor's wife, others claimed their attempts to barge to the front of the queue in the kitchen area infuriated others while one of the airmen said Milns had squared up to him first.

Within seconds, Milns was laid out unconscious on the floor and Beaumont, who had been sitting next to him, was also on the ground, doubled up after being stabbed in the stomach.

Five out of six witnesses called to give evidence during the trial at Leeds Assizes identified Corporal James Jordan as the man who stabbed Beaumont with an eight-inch long clasp knife which had a spring-loaded blade activated by a button.

Although there was only one stab wound, prosecutor Mr Peter Stanley-Price sought to convince the jury that all four Americans had carried out a concerted attack. He backed this up with witnesses who claimed all four had stood over Beaumont and repeatedly kicked him in the stomach after the stabbing. Others spoke of at least two other airmen carrying knives.

But the case against three of the men dramatically collapsed on the trial's fourth day.

The court had already heard details of a statement made by the eldest of the men, Leroy Grayson, while in custody awaiting committal. In it, he said he had asked to see a priest for advice after hoping that one of his compatriots would have come forward to tell the truth.

Grayson said his statement was intended to clear two other innocent men as well as himself and he went on to identify Jordan as the one carrying the knife.

Further submissions from defence counsel convinced the Judge, Mr Justice Byrne, to direct not guilty verdicts on Grayson, Vincent Hill and James Martin on the grounds of insufficient evidence.

Jordan was now left alone in the dock, his co-accused shaking him by the hand and patting his shoulder as he passed by them on his way to the witness box immediately after the case against them had been dismissed.

Referred to as 'Diamond Jim' by one of the female witnesses from the cafe, Jordan had recently celebrated his 21st birthday in prison awaiting the trial. Originally from Newark, New Jersey, and one of eight children, he had left high school at 17 intending to study at university. Instead he volunteered for the forces a year later and was posted to England, originally being stationed in Lincolnshire.

Little did he know it but he was about to make history as the first American serviceman to face a capital charge in this country since United States forces returned here in 1951 and came under the jurisdiction of the British courts a year later.

Giving evidence, Jordan said he punched one man who had charged towards him and then struck another, holding the knife in his fist with the blade closed. He said he had no idea why the men tried to attack him but hinted at the undoubted racial tension of the day by adding there were several pubs in Hull in which he had been asked to leave.

The jury were asked to decide if the stabbing was intentional or justified in the circumstances. Just over three hours later they found Jordan guilty of murder, with the foreman asking that the jury's "strong recommendation for mercy" be recorded.

Mr Justice Byrne donned the traditional black cap to pass the death sentence as Jordan, flanked by three prison officers, stared straight back at him without showing any sign of emotion.

At the time, the death penalty was rarely being carried out and public opposition to it was becoming increasingly vociferous. Indeed, at the beginning of the American's trial, a jury member was replaced after she informed the court she had previously signed a petition against capital punishment.

In reality, there was little likelihood of Jordan ever facing the noose, especially as Mr Justice Byrne had also commented on the jury's recommendation for mercy when passing sentence. Even so, his fate remained unclear until four days after his conviction when the case took an unusual and dramatic twist.

The defence counsel had already discounted any appeal against the sentence when a letter arrived from a doctor who had observed Beaumont's treatment in hospital and disagreed with the cause of death being simply attributed to the stab wound.

Dr Keith Simpson, a pathologist at Hull Royal Infirmary, claimed that although the wound was not trivial, it had not been sufficient enough to cause the death of an otherwise fit and healthy young man. Furthermore, he criticised the use of an antibiotic drug, terramcyin, in the treatment of Beaumont.

The drug was used to kill dangerous bacteria in the body or prevent bacteria multiplying. An attendant danger was that the remaining bacteria might thrive and multiply at a faster rate than if the drug had not been used.

Dr Simpson claimed Beaumont had already displayed initial intolerance to the drug and said treatment should have stopped then. That it did not, he added, was "palpably wrong". The doctor said Beaumont had contracted a particular type of bronchial pneumonia associated with the use of terramcyin and it was this which had caused his death rather than the stab wound.

This new evidence was backed by a surgeon at the hospital, Guy Blackburn, who had also witnessed Beaumont's treatment. He also considered the wound had been less than life-threatening and claimed restoring the use of the drug in Beaumont's case had been extremely hazardous.

He went on to say the doses injected on each of the last two days before death had been "grossly excessive".

With this new substantial doubt over whether the stab wound had caused the death, three Appeal Court judges had little hesitation in taking the rare step of allowing additional evidence to be heard when the case came before them exactly a month after

Jordan's conviction.

The defence called both Dr Simpson and Mr Blackburn to give evidence and concluded that an "error of judgement" had been made in the hospital treatment. The appeal judges ruled that this evidence should have been placed before the jury. The fact that it was unknown at the time, they added, did not reflect badly on either the prosecution or the defence.

Mr Justice Hallett said it had never occurred to the prosecution, defence, trial judge or jury to question if the stabbing was the cause of death because they had no reason to think otherwise on the evidence presented to them at the time. "We feel that if the jury had heard two doctors of the standing of Dr Simpson and Mr Blackburn giving the same evidence they might have hesitated very long before saying that they were satisfied that death was due to the stab wound," he said.

The judges unanimously upheld the appeal and Jordan's sentence was duly quashed. The burly and bespectacled airman grinned broadly as he left the famous London court building a free man.

The fresh evidence which had helped overturn his conviction led to an inquiry by the regional hospital authority into the treatment given to Beaumont during his eight days in the infirmary.

Three independent medical assessors were appointed to carry out the inquiry and they turned the affair on its head once again by concluding: "This man's life was unsavable and his death was not in any way attributable to the treatment he received in hospital".

The assessors said they believed Beaumont had been "on the point of death" on the fifth post-operative day when the police had been advised by a surgeon to take a bedside statement in case he never recovered. "The fact that Beaumont survived for a further three days was due, in our opinion, to the energetic and competent methods used by the hospital," they added.

Satisfied with the findings, the regional hospital board gave its backing to the infirmary's nursing and medical staff by expressing full confidence in their actions. The matter was officially closed even if it still left many unanswered questions.

In Seaton Street an elderly woman in an overcoat and headscarf pushed a trolley filled with coal and firewood into her home, sat down in her small front living-room and answered questions from reporters as best she could.

"All this business has got me down," said Mrs Sarah Beaumont. "I will get to know what killed my son even if I have to get him out of his grave to do it." Despite her brave words, she never did.

MURDERS OF HULL

'TIL DEATH US DO PART

✝

E tty Forsey should have been the happiest woman in the world. Married for just four days, her husband had a secure job and she was busily sorting out their new home. But her Sunday morning wedding, in St Paul's Church in Hull, had been held in secret without the knowledge or blessing of her father. Moses Witty, who worked as a coal dealer, had regarded Etty — or Rosetta to give her full name — as his favourite daughter. The eldest child in a large family, she had effectively run the Witty household for over eight years since her mother became a bedridden invalid. When she was 24 she met Harry Forsey, a fireman at Reckitts. It was 1900 and after years of self-sacrifice Etty believed she was about to embark on a romance which would lead to wedded bliss.

Her father, however, was both furious and alarmed that Etty was considering a marriage which would take her away from the family home. Her blossoming relationship with Harry was soon causing heated arguments in the Witty household between father and daughter and when the young couple got engaged a year later, Witty openly forbid her to marry.

Despite this hostility, it later emerged he had bought a clock, sewing machine and a dressing table as wedding gifts for his daughter.

Only aware of his opposition to her wishes, Etty eventually moved out, going to live with a relative for a few weeks before the secret wedding at a church deliberately chosen because of its distance from her parents' house off Sculcoates Lane. Her departure plunged Witty into depression and on one occasion he stormed to Forsey's mother's home and told her he would rather kill himself than see his daughter marry her son. Little did Eliza Forsey realise at the time that his threat was far from hollow.

On the Thursday following their marriage, Etty had taken her husband's dinner to his workplace in Dansom Lane before returning to their new terraced home off St Mark's Street. As she washed some dishes there was a knock at the back door. Opening the door with a wet saucer still in one hand, she let out a scream as her father stood in front of her with a pistol aimed straight at her head.

The sound of two shots fired in quick succession startled neighbours who rushed to the scene, one unknowingly brushing past Witty as he calmly made his getaway. In the Forsey's back yard they found Etty lying dead in a pool of blood with two clearly visible wounds to her head.

Witty, meanwhile, was walking to Harry Forsey's mother's home in Nicholson Street, just over a mile from where he had shot his daughter. When Mrs Forsey answered the knock on her door, she found Witty standing on her step holding out a note which he said was from Etty.

As Mrs Forsey reached out for the note Witty pulled his revolver from a pocket and shouted: "I have shot Etty. I told you I would do for the lot of you," before firing again, wounding her in the hip and knocking her off balance as she staggered into the back kitchen. The shot alerted her husband Frank, who had been upstairs at the time, and within seconds he was trying to wrestle Witty to the ground. Two more shots rang out — one hitting a door and the other a stool — before he was finally overpowered with the help of two neighbours.

The police were at the house within minutes but had not bargained for Witty attempting to carry out the threat made to Mrs Forsey several weeks earlier. Asking for a bucket because he said he was going to be sick, Witty suddenly produced a razor from his pocket and slashed his own throat in front of the shocked onlookers.

The 49-year-old lapsed into unconsciousness and very nearly died from his self-inflicted wound, spending 11 weeks in Hull Royal Infirmary before he was considered well enough to stand trial. In the meantime, Etty Forsey had been buried — exactly a week after getting married.

Witty was charged with the murder of his daughter and the attempted murder of her mother-in-law. In a barely audible voice because of his throat wound he pleaded not guilty. His defence maintained he had been mentally unbalanced at the time of the shootings because of his depression over his daughter's departure. The jury returned a guilty verdict but said the murder had been committed while Witty had been of an unsound mind.

The Lord Chief Justice, the Rt Hon Richard Everard, who was presiding at York Assizes, agreed and passed what was effectively a life sentence by ordering that Witty be detained at His Majesty's pleasure.

The circumstances behind Etty Forsey's death at the hands of her father were undoubtedly unusual and shocking but not altogether surprising as crimes of passion are invariably triggered, sooner or later, by the act of marriage.

Like young Etty, June Stevenson's dreams of a long and happy marriage were also short-lived, in her case not managing to last more than half an hour.

After marrying Graham Stevenson at Hull Register Office, the couple returned to her parents' home for a small family reception to celebrate the happy event. It might have been Friday the 13th, but June was determined to make sure the day was a memorable one, carrying a corsage of flowers decorated around a horse shoe for good luck. However, a knock on the door turned it into a nightmare for all concerned as a team of police officers walked in and promptly arrested her new husband. Within a few hours the bridegroom was facing a murder charge.

Graham Stevenson, a 21-year-old labourer, had casually told June's father shortly before the ceremony that he had found a dead body earlier that morning in the back garden of a house next door to where the couple were intending to set up home in Woodcock Street.

Stevenson had given the same information to a policeman he met as he made his way to the Register Office that morning. With hindsight, it seems incredible that he was allowed to leave the area after giving a brief statement saying he knew nothing about the body.

As it was, while detectives and forensic experts began piecing together the last movements of an apparently strangled teenage girl, the man who killed her was smiling for his wedding day photographs.

Margaret Wainfer was an only child and, at 16, a typical teenager. She had left school a year earlier and, after a brief spell working, was unemployed, earning pocket money by babysitting for neighbours in Arundel Street where she lived with her parents. After her death, they described her as a quiet girl who did not have a boyfriend.

But girlfriends told a different story. They said she wanted to leave home and move in with a boyfriend. She was also going out dancing in clubs and had developed a reputation for flirting with boys.

The last her father, Fred, had seen of her was on the Thursday afternoon that week when his daughter said she wanted to go out and see a friend on Holderness Road. The unemployed docker gave her 10p and she was gone.

Margaret ended up visiting a 16-year-old girl who lived across the city in the Boulevard. The girl had become her best friend in recent months and that night Margaret confided in her that she thought she might be pregnant. She asked to stay the night there but her girlfriend's parents refused. Margaret reluctantly left only to miss the last bus home from Hessle Road.

The teenager sat in a bus shelter not really knowing what to do when a policeman saw her and asked what she was doing. Margaret told her unhappy story but eventually agreed with his advice that she should make her way home. At that moment Graham Stevenson walked by and asked the officer what time it was.

It had just turned midnight and Stevenson was on his way back to Woodcock Street after a stag night spent drinking on Hessle Road. The constable later recalled Stevenson had looked at the girl in the bus shelter as he stopped to ask the time but walked off without talking to her.

At first, Stevenson told the police he had never even seen the girl before but quickly changed his story, claiming she had waved to him from the bus shelter as the policeman strolled off. Telling him she had nowhere to go, he said he agreed she could stay at his house but only if she slept in the back bedroom and was out of the house by 6am because of his wedding. "I didn't want any hanky-panky," he told detectives.

At the house, he claimed she went upstairs but re-appeared half-dressed, laughing as she teased him by waving her tights in his face. Stevenson said he just snapped, pressing her neck hard with his thumbs before she went numb and fell to the floor. He claimed he then blacked out, saying he could not recall tying the tights around her neck. However, he did remember trying to revive her with a mouthful of milk before dragging her outside and tipping her over the garden fence.

The medical and forensic evidence being gathered by the police painted a slightly different picture. Fibres from the girl's clothes were found in the house and on the garden fence while the position the body was found in suggested it had been casually dropped from some height. The post mortem established the cause of death was asphyxia due to strangulation, both manually and by ligature. The tights had been knotted so tightly around the girl's neck that a doctor could not get his finger in between to loosen them.

Margaret also had cuts to her chest and bruises to her arm and foot. Although Stevenson denied having sex with her, the pathologist who examined the body also found evidence of recent sexual intercourse. The police already knew that apart from the half-hour spent at Stevenson's home before her death, the teenager had been with a girlfriend for the best part of the afternoon and night.

At his trial in December 1971, Stevenson pleaded not guilty to murder. The prosecution maintained that while his statements came somewhere near to the truth, they were not a full and honest disclosure of what actually happened that night.

Prosecuting, Mr Gilbert Gray alleged the couple had sex only for Stevenson to kill the girl when she threatened to tell of their night together. He pressed home his case by focusing on the force used to strangle the girl with her own tights, which had been knotted with two bows tied to the knot itself. The defence's argument of provocation, he maintained, was no excuse for what Stevenson did.

The trial lasted little over a day and the jury took just over two hours to return a guilty verdict by an 11 to 1 majority. As Stevenson was led grim-faced from the dock to start a life sentence he caught sight of his wife in the public gallery and shouted: "Ta-ra, love!". Mrs Stevenson burst into tears and left court being comforted by friends and relatives. Within six months the bride whose marriage effectively ended after half-an-hour was filing for divorce.

MURDERS OF HULL

KILLER
ON THE LOOSE

✝

T oday Hull Marina is one of the city's main tourist attractions, a haven for pleasure boat owners and those out for an enjoyable afternoon stroll. Perhaps the only reminder of how the area was barely 30 years ago is Humber Street where fruit traders still go about the bustling early morning business of dispatching their goods from small warehouses standing shoulder to shoulder on the pavement. In the 1960s the nearby dock which is now full of yachts was witnessing a slow but steady decline and the surrounding area was beginning to reflect that change. A maze of streets and alleys were dotted with old pubs and dimly-lit coffee bars before giving way to the comparative splendour of Victoria Pier and the berthing point for the Hull to New Holland ferry.

During a routine early morning patrol one Sunday in May 1966, PC Cyril Renton shone his torch to pierce the darkness in one of these narrow lanes. He had done exactly the same over two hours earlier, just before 1am, but had seen nothing. Now, looking down the lane from its other end, he could make out something on the ground. It was the dead body of a young girl.

The lane still runs between Humber Street and Blanket Row and although it has no official name locals know it as Pig Alley, no doubt derived from two former slaughterhouses which once operated along the alley. Although used mainly as a simple cut-through, the alley stands near the site of some of the earliest working class dwellings to be built in 19th century Hull, typified by their design around tiny courts. Although Pig Alley remains, the last example of the houses in it were sadly demolished in 1993.

The girl was lying on her back near a wall with her head twisted to one side. Even in torchlight, it was obvious she had suffered serious head injuries.

Detectives hauled out of their beds knew a difficult job lay ahead. The girl had been found in a remote area where potential witnesses were likely to be thin on the ground. There were no immediate clues left by her killer in the alley or in the surrounding streets and they faced having to trace the last moments of a teenage girl over the course of a Saturday night.

When 15-year-old Margaret Lowson's identity became known their job wasn't made much easier. She had left her home on Hessle Road late the previous afternoon saying she was hoping to meet a friend. If she didn't, she told her mother and stepfather she would probably go to the cinema on her own.

Her family knew her as a quiet girl with few friends. She was the youngest of three children and the family had only recently moved to Hull from Bradford, where her eldest brother remained because of his job. Once Margaret had left school that Easter she started work as a fish packer. The day before she was last seen alive she had drawn her first full week's wages, spending some of her money on her first ever pair of stockings.

Margaret's name was, however, known to the police, having once previously been reported as missing from home. It was this link which initially identified her and police officers broke the news to her family later that morning, her stepfather having already been out twice looking for her.

With the family unable to provide a major breakthrough, the police took the momentous step of calling in Scotland Yard to help investigate the case.

It was the first time Scotland Yard officers had been called in on a Hull crime probe since tool merchant Oswald Walker was found murdered in his George Street shop in 1936. Walker had died from blows which broke every bone in his head and he was also partially strangled by his own collar. Robbery was believed to be the motive as his wallet was missing but no-one was ever caught and charged over his death.

Thirty years later, the then Hull City Police Force still had only a handful of detectives with sufficient expertise to handle a difficult and potentially large murder inquiry. A measure of the importance attached to such a crime in those days was demonstrated by the Chief Constable, Robert Walton, interrupting a long weekend break on Tyneside to drive back to Hull to oversee events. Officers from the Regional Crime Squad were drafted in as a matter of routine for major investigations but Scotland Yard detectives were still considered to be the ultimate specialists in unsolved murder.

Another attraction for the local force was that calling in Scotland Yard cost nothing — providing the request was made within 48 hours of the crime being committed. Under this rule, all accommodation, living and travel expenses were met by the Yard.

As the Hull murder team awaited the arrival of the Yard men, they set about the huge task of visiting every ship in port to check every man who had been ashore that weekend. To complicate matters, the Royal Navy guided missile ship, HMS Agincourt, was in port on a courtesy visit while a Danish Navy frigate was also berthed in King George Dock. Both were visited and the Danish vessel was allowed to sail for Copenhagen early on Monday morning.

A post-mortem suggested the teenager had been dead for around three hours before being discovered. The blows to her head were probably caused by a fist, or possibly a shoe, but no weapon had been found. From the position of the body police concluded it was likely she had been struck from behind but had also put up a struggle. Money scattered around the scene belonged to her and it was suggested she might have left scratch marks on her attacker's face.

The arrival of Detective Superintendent Leslie Rouse from Scotland Yard to lead the investigation co-incided with the departure of two Hull detectives to Denmark to question seamen from the frigate which had earlier been allowed to leave the port. With them was an African sailor who had come forward to say he had seen the girl with two seamen in a dockside cafe on the night of her death. As it turned out, their enquiries drew a blank and another promising lead dissolved.

In the days following the murder the 40-strong team of detectives and officers working on the case patiently followed dozens of similar leads. A girl roughly fitting Margaret's description was said to have been seen with a coloured man who had his arm around her walking along Castle Street. Another witness said he saw a girl similar to Margaret walking alone by Prince's Dock at 7.30pm. In the two pubs nearest to the murder scene — the Humber Dock Tavern and the Navigation Inn — no-one had seen a girl looking like Margaret that night. Someone matching her description was seen sitting on the pier but interviews with passengers on the late-night ferry again got the police nowhere.

The most certain identification was given by a man who claimed he saw her walking in Queens Gardens at about 7.30pm. He said he followed her for a while as she walked first to the bus station and then to Porter Street.

Despite taking over 500 statements in two weeks, the police still could not establish why Margaret had been in the Old Town or even where she had been in the hours leading up to her death. Det Supt Rouse was faced with the problem of trying to read the mind of a quiet, reserved girl with hardly any friends who rarely went out.

Forensic evidence which showed that Margaret had a meal between 10 and 10.30pm on the night she was killed gave detectives fresh hope. They believed someone must have bought it for her because she had not spent any of her own money. Cafes and restaurants which had already been checked were visited again but to no avail.

After ten weeks, the two Scotland Yard detectives brought in to lead Hull's biggest-ever murder inquiry were heading back to London empty-handed. It did not mean the case was closed but the move acknowledged the fact it was being wound down, with fewer than a dozen officers still working from the inquiry room set up at the Queens Gardens station.

Det Supt Rouse maintained someone was shielding the killer and predicted: "One day the man who killed her will drop a careless word which will lead the police to him". In the vast majority of murder cases, the killer is arrested with the first 72 hours.

In November, some six months after Margaret's death, Rouse returned to Hull to give evidence at the inquest. The jury's verdict that she was murdered by a person or persons unknown was a sad formality and the only new evidence to surface at the hearing was that there had been an attempted sexual assault on the girl during the attack. This fact had long been known to the police but they had decided to keep it from the press. Within days of the inquest a dramatic development in the case would be handled in the same way.

Margaret's stepfather, George Shadforth, had also given evidence at the inquest, telling how he had twice gone out looking for her before being picked up by a police car and driven to the mortuary for the grim task of identifying her body.

A few days after the hearing he received a letter addressed to him in unfamiliar handwriting and postmarked in Hull. It read: "I see the stupid police have not found the murderer of your daughter yet. I have killed once and I will kill again. Yes, I murdered your daughter. She found out to her cost that no girl can resist me and live. No-one will find me out, not even the big shot 'tec from Scotland Yard." It was signed: "From the murderer of your daughter".

Almost every long-running unsolved murder case attracts hoaxers, perhaps the most famous in recent years being the tape recording sent to detectives investigating the so-called Yorkshire Ripper murders in 1979. Hoax letters had already complicated what was the largest manhunt ever mounted by British police when the tape arrived to throw the entire inquiry into confusion.

Senior detectives were convinced it was the killer and broadcast it to the nation. For months they tried to match a suspect with the Wearside accent identified on the tape. During that period, Peter Sutcliffe was interviewed for a second time by the police only to be dismissed for not having a Wearside accent like the one on the tape.

When George Shadforth took his letter to the police they also took it seriously but for good reason as it bore a striking similarity to another recent letter sent to a young girl in Hull which had been passed on to them. Seemingly in the same handwriting but even more obscene, it had opened: "I have murdered one girl, you are the next. Before I kill you I am going to torture you." It was signed: "The Psychopath".

Realising the likely hysteria if their suspicions were made public, the police kept these new details to themselves as other letters with the same handwriting began to emerge. One, written to the mother of a young girl, read: "I have already murdered one girl. Your daughter is next. I have seen her two or three times and she is a so pretty girl. You have been warned. The Psychopath."

Another, posted to a single girl living in Hessle, was equally chilling. "I am going to kill you," it read. "I won't do it right away. I want to see you suffer first. Like the last girl I killed. She was only 15. I made her suffer first. I like doing that. I hate all women. I shall probably use my favourite knife on you."

Frustratingly, the police could not establish a common link between the girls who received the letters which might have revealed who was behind them. As the weeks and months passed they seemed no nearer to finding Margaret Lowson's killer.

In October 1967 — nearly 17 months after her murder — shop assistant Sandra Carr returned home to her lodgings in Louis Street in Hull after a day's work. The attractive 17-year-old blonde had a boyfriend but this fact had not deterred a fellow lodger from pestering her for a date.

The man, it seemed to her, was an unlikely suitor. Not only was he probably twice her age, but he also wore a wig and was partially deaf. Moreover, the bachelor's manner made her feel uneasy, seemingly oblivious to her efforts to ignore his three previous requests to go out with him. In short, Samuel Stephenson made her flesh creep.

That night he was there again, standing by her door after she came home from work, asking if she was going dancing that evening. Sandra went for tea and on returning to her room she heard a noise and saw her bedspread move. Picking up a paper knife she edged across to the bed and saw two feet sticking out from underneath. She kicked the bed in terror only for Stephenson to appear from under it and grab her by the hair. Wielding a knife of his own he slashed at her hair before knocking her to the floor and kicking her in the face.

During the struggle Stephenson's wig fell off and Sandra would later say that at one stage he appeared to be in a sort of trance. Seeing her chance to escape, she climbed through an open window, jumped from a drainpipe and ran for help with blood pouring from three small knife wounds to her neck.

As the teenager was being taken to hospital, Stephenson walked to a nearby police box on Princes Avenue nursing a cut to his arm. He told officers he had just knifed a girl he only knew as Sandra at an address in Louis Street and then went on to admit committing a similar offence in East Park four months earlier.

On that occasion, two sisters, aged 15 and seven, had been startled by a man wielding a knife who had grabbed the elder girl by the throat before running off when the younger sister started screaming.

The 33-year-old unemployed labourer was taken to Hull's Central Police Station for further questioning. As he was being put into a cell he said he had something else to tell the police about. Recalling his own birthday on May 14 the previous year, Stephenson went on to give astonished officers a detailed account of how he had killed Margaret Lowson.

He said he had been in the Earl de Grey pub that night when he first saw her walking past in the street outside. Deciding to follow her, he stalked the teenager until she reached Pig Alley, which Stephenson thought was a dead-end.

"If she had not put up a struggle I would not have bashed her, but she did," he went on.

"I hit her with my fists and left her there, and then I ran away."

His description of the attack and the position of the girl's body convinced detectives they had found the killer at last and a search of his flat confirmed their belief. In a drawer police found a number of obscene and threatening letters which Stephenson had written and placed in addressed envelopes ready for posting. One letter was addressed to Det Supt James Cocksworth, head of Hull's CID, and was signed: "From the killer of Margaret Lowson". The room was also littered with detective magazines and books on infamous murder cases, including Jack the Ripper.

Over a series of interviews, Stephenson admitted killing the teenager and writing all the "Psychopath' letters, including the one sent to Margaret's stepfather.

Det Supt Rouse travelled from Scotland Yard for the committal to read a statement by Stephenson which said he had confessed because he was frightened of killing again. In the highly-charged atmosphere of the courtroom, the detective who first arrested Stephenson fainted as the transcript of his evidence was read back to him and re-appeared only after a short break to recover.

At the subsequent trial, Stephenson was ordered to be detained indefinitely at the Rampton mental hospital after the prosecution accepted his guilty plea to manslaughter on the grounds of diminished responsibility.

Opening the case, prosecutor Rudolph Lyons unwittingly bracketed Stephenson with one of his heroes by comparing him to Jack the Ripper as a man "too shy to make normal contacts with women, becoming sex-obsessed and ultimately committing physical violence".

A psychiatric report revealed a family history of nervous breakdowns and a head injury at the age of four which had led to a series of black-outs in later life. Evacuated from Hull to a farm during the Second World War, Stephenson had told how starting fires in fields and hurting animals excited him as a child. Labelling Stephenson as "an extremely dangerous man", the psychiatrist concluded that he obtained sexual pleasure through fantasy, often flavoured with sadistic overtones, and observed he had shown no remorse at all about his crimes.

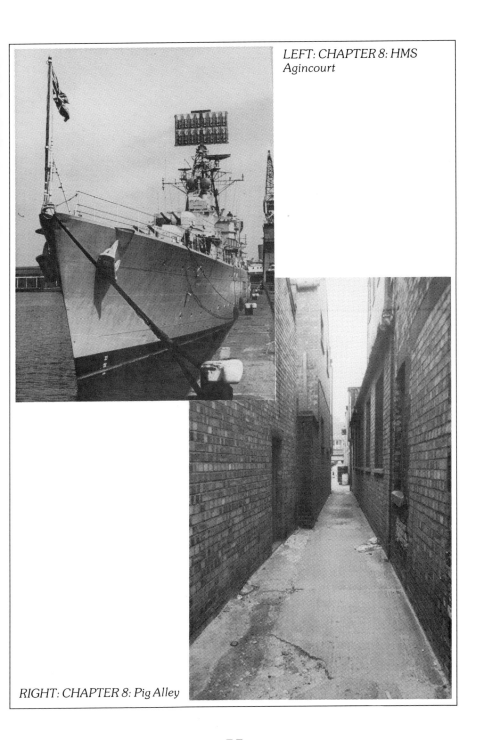

LEFT: CHAPTER 8: HMS Agincourt

RIGHT: CHAPTER 8: Pig Alley

ABOVE: CHAPTER 9: Police search where Leslie Hutchinson's body was found (Donald Innes)

LEFT: CHAPTER 9: Leslie Hutchinson.

RIGHT: CHAPTER 9: Marjorie Hutchinson.

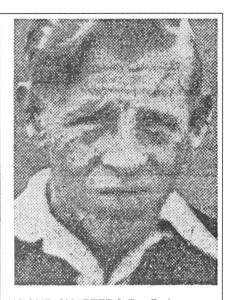

ABOVE: CHAPTER 9: Roy Bigby.

LEFT: CHAPTER 9: Kenneth Green (Donald Innes).

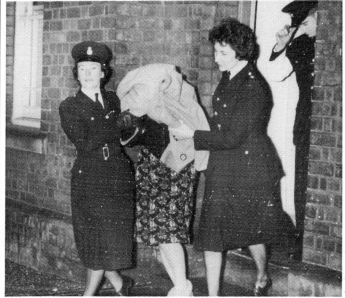

LEFT:CHAPTER 9: The arrest of Marjorie Hitchinson.

ABOVE: CHAPTER 10: Police search Bransholme tip for the body of Carol Rodgers.

LEFT: CHAPTER 10: Carol Rodgers.

LEFT: CHAPTER 10: Ada Foxton.

ABOVE: CHAPTER 10: Geoffrey Middleton.

RIGHT: CHAPTER 10: Weapons used by Frank Marritt.

ABOVE: CHAPTER 10:
Police search at Geoffrey
Middleton's former flat.

ABOVE: CHAPTER 11: The Wensley Lodge fire.

RIGHT: CHAPTER 11: Bruce Lee.

*LEFT: CHAPTER 11:
Bruce Lee after being
sentenced.*

*LEFT: CHAPTER 11:
Ron Sagar.*

*BELOW: CHAPTER 12:
Derek Rose.*

ABOVE: CHAPTER 12: Ann Widdowson.

ABOVE: CHAPTER 12: Cyril Olsen.

LEFT: CHAPTER 12: Christine Acey.

84

HIRED TO KILL

✝

If the Lowson case was eventually solved almost by accident, copybook detective work was responsible for cracking one of the area's most sensational murder investigations of this century. Once again Scotland Yard men were involved but this was four years before the Pig Alley murder and just outside the city boundary in the neighbouring town of Hessle, which was then policed by the old East Riding force. Two Yard men were called in after the body of 40-year-old welder Leslie Hutchinson had been found battered and strangled in a lonely lane near to where he owned a boarding kennels. He had been discovered late at night by his business partner, Roy Bigby, who kept poultry on a smallholding next to the kennels. Bigby initially called the police to report a road accident. Hutchinson had been lying in a pool of blood next to his motorcycle.

Despite it being dark, the police soon realised it was more than just an accident. His extensive head injuries suggested a sustained attack of heavy blows while the cloth belt from his denim overalls had been wrapped twice around his mouth and neck and then fastened using the buckle. There was also evidence to suggest he had been dragged and carried some distance from the motorcycle as traces of blood were found several feet away from both the body and the bike. Because he was a burly man, it seemed likely that more than one person had been involved in the crime.

Daylight would reveal another sinister clue in the shape of a wire which had seemingly been tied to a tree and pulled across the lane, presumably to knock the motorcyclist from his machine.

His 39-year-old wife, Marjorie, was woken at their Buttfield Avenue home in Hessle and told the news. Despite being upset, she gave police another clue and soon detectives were confident enough to state that £31 in £5 and £1 notes had been stolen from the dead man's wallet that night. The chances that these notes might be bloodstained offered hope that someone might remember seeing one.

Mrs Hutchinson worked during the day at the kennels while her husband took jobs as a shipyard welder, returning to work nights and weekends at Fulstryde Kennels. She told police she had given her husband his tea at a small caravan on the site before returning home to get ready for a Thursday night out at Hull Fair with a group of friends, including Roy Bigby. Coming home after the Fair to find her husband missing, she said she had not been concerned because he would often sleep overnight in the caravan if he had been working there late.

The Hutchinsons were known to the police at Hessle because of their past domestic disputes. Mrs Hutchinson had sought police protection from her husband on several previous occasions, claiming he regularly beat her. She had even obtained three separation orders through the courts on the grounds of cruelty, as well as one on the grounds of her husband's desertion. She had also walked out, once going to live in the caravan at the kennels with their young son. Each separation, however, was followed by a reconciliation.

When told her husband had probably been murdered and asked if she knew anyone who might have committed the crime, she reeled off a list of women he had openly boasted of sleeping with.

Roy Bigby, a 35-year-old former tugboat cook, confirmed Mrs Hutchinson's statement. He said he had hired a van to take the group of friends to Hull Fair and called in at the kennels on the way home to check his geese and hens as the site had been broken into recently. His headlights had picked out the motorcycle and he then saw his partner lying near the bottom of a hedge which separated the lane from a railway embankment. He said he immediately turned back and went for the police.

Robbery was an unlikely motive for such a seemingly calculated crime and detectives were initially hindered by the murder scene itself, a remote spot hugging the railway line near to Hessle Station. Fulstryde Kennels were at the end of a track leading from Woodfield Lane, between Ferriby Road and the banks of the River Humber. No-one lived nearby and looking for the murder weapon in the dense undergrowth was like searching for a needle in a haystack.

Led by the Yard's Det Supt John Bailey, the 60-strong murder team included detectives from Hull City as well as the East Riding. On paper at least, their two most likely suspects — Marjorie Hutchinson and Roy Bigby — had seemingly watertight alibis, being with a party at the Fair that night. Even so, a search of Mrs Hutchinson's fireplace had revealed a heel plate and several charred pieces of boot. The police were well aware a pathologist had concluded that some of Leslie Hutchinson's head injuries could have been caused by a kick from a boot.

As news of the murder emerged, owners began to arrive at the scene to take their dogs back home while police started trying to trace everyone who had recent dealings there. Eliminating people from a police inquiry, however remote the connection, could sometimes reap rich rewards.

The Hutchinsons kept six of their own Alsatian dogs at the kennels and two days after the killing Mrs Hutchinson took two of her favourite dogs, Dusk Fulstryde and Emperor, to the Hull Alsatian Show, winning two first prizes. "The police advised her to go," her son Leslie told reporters, "mainly to take her mind off things".

Two days later she gave a police statement which referred to an incident earlier in the month when her husband had been startled by a mystery prowler at the kennels. One theory put to the police by Mrs Hutchinson was that the intruder might have been trying to exact some kind of revenge after a row over a puppy.

Four months earlier, Dusk the Alsatian had given birth to a litter of pups. One was immediately christened Fluffybags because of his exceptionally long fawn and black coat, which not only marked him apart from the rest of the litter but automatically ruled out any plans to enter him at a show dog. Detectives learned the pup was initially sold for £8 but returned the same day because the buyer's wife did not like him. Mrs Hutchinson said the dog was then sold to a man who she could only remember as being called Mr Brown. Again, the fluffy pup had been brought back she said, but her husband had refused to give a refund and the man had stormed off leaving the dog once more at the kennels. Questioned separately, Roy Bigby thought the man's name had been Fred Brown.

A book in Mr Hutchinson's handwriting contained an entry referring to a man called Brown at a Hull address which, when checked by the police, turned out to be fictitious.

Fluffybag's current owners were traced in East Hull. They had bought him at the kennels ten days before Leslie Hutchinson met his death. Now, over a week since the murder, Det Supt Bailey took the calculated gamble of having a photograph of Fluffybags featured in the Hull Daily Mail with an appeal for information about the mystery man called Brown who had owned the pup for a week. Within hours of publication, an anonymous telephone call to Hessle police station had detectives eagerly checking their files.

The man identified by the caller was Fred Green, a meat porter from Hull. The 34-year-old worked for a firm which was used regularly by Mrs Hutchinson to buy bones for the dogs at her kennels.

Green was arrested that night in the Portland Arms pub in Hull and quizzed about the dog. He agreed he had owned the pup but claimed he found it wandering in the Porter Street area of Hull and eventually turned it loose again because it was making a mess. Taken to Hessle police station, he maintained his story but admitted knowing Marjorie Hutchinson through her daily visits to his workplace.

Despite Green's statement, detectives were certain he was the mysterious Mr Brown and the next day interviewed his wife as well as work colleagues and the licensee of his local, the Portland Arms. They also found a freshly-washed but still blood-stained towel at his home which his wife could not identify. Twenty four hours later he was back at Hessle station giving detectives a graphic account of Leslie Hutchinson's last moments. The pieces of the jigsaw began falling into place as Green admitted carrying out the attack with Bigby and told police he had been paid by Marjorie Hutchinson to kill her husband.

While Green was showing police a large unlit bonfire site where he had thrown a piece of lead-filled hosepipe used in the attack, Bigby was being shown Green's confession. Turning pale and trembling badly, he looked up and said: "That's it then, isn't it". Det Supt Bailey then waited for Marjorie Hutchinson to be brought in. At first she maintained her story until being shown the statements of Green and Bigby. Re-reading passages, she mumbled: "I did not intend to have him killed. I only wanted him to have a good hiding."

Nearly a fortnight after the crime, Green, Bigby and Mrs Hutchinson appeared charged with murder before a special session of the South Hunsley Beacon Sessions court, specially switched to the Guildhall law courts in Hull for the occasion. The courtroom and public gallery were packed, mainly by women eager to glimpse the still rare sight of a member of their own sex facing a murder charge.

At their trial in late January 1963, Bigby and Mrs Hutchinson denied murdering her husband but Green pleaded guilty and was jailed for life. He was then recalled to court to give evidence for the prosecution against his two co-accused.

Green had been an unlikely hired assassin. An alcoholic who spent most of his money on drink, he got to know of Marjorie Hutchinson's marital problems by the frequent sight of cuts and bruises to her face when she appeared for her bones at his firm. She made no secret of it and openly told anyone there who would listen that her husband was to blame for her injuries.

Bigby frequently accompanied Mrs Hutchinson on her daily trips for meat and bones in the weeks before her husband's death because they were now lovers. The married father-of-four had known Leslie Hutchinson for years. After becoming a partner, he saw the fights between the Hutchinsons at first hand but never intervened. His own marriage was also in turmoil and he had moved out of his Ash Grove home, off Brighton Street in Hull, going to live at the kennels. After years of being taunted by her husband over his affairs with other women, Marjorie Hutchinson and Roy Bigby were now having secret sex sessions in the tiny caravan at Fulstryde.

Following one particularly brutal beating, she had asked Green if he could do a "job" for her. At the trial, she insisted this only meant a beating of equal force to the one handed out to her but Green was equally adamant she wanted her husband dead.

Other witnesses from the meat firm backed him up, saying she frequently talked of "wanting rid" of him.

Green accepted the offer on condition that he was paid. At first he saw it as easy money, being paid small amounts for not actually doing anything. On four different occasions he was paid but returned from the kennels without having come close to harming his intended victim.

As well as being the mystery prowler who had startled Mr Hutchinson just weeks before his death, he had also posed as the bogus Mr Brown to buy Fluffybags the pup with £12 given to him by Mrs Hutchinson. Somewhat typically, he bought the pup for £7 and kept the rest for himself. Buying the dog had supposedly been an excuse to get near Mr Hutchinson but Green ducked out of his promised assault. On another occasion, nerves again got the better of him while hiding behind a shed at the kennels and he ran off still clutching an unused hammer.

On the day of the scheduled trip to Hull Fair, Mrs Hutchinson asked Green to do the "job" that night, announcing she and Bigby had drawn up a plan. It started with the trip wire being fixed across the path and ended with the arrangements to join regulars at the Albert Hall pub for the evening outing to the Fair.

Timing was essential to Marjorie Hutchinson's plan. She knew her husband would come to the caravan at 6.30pm for his tea. In the half-hour before then she had to pick up Green in Hull, drop him and Bigby off in Hessle Square and return to finish cooking the vegetables. When her husband was having his tea, Bigby and Green would fix the trip wire and wait, with all three hoping that no unexpected caller would come up the lane.

She arrived back at the caravan five minutes before her husband. He stormed in angry about his wages, claiming they were £4 short. His temper continued to boil during the meal and afterwards he grabbed his wife in the way she knew he wanted to make love. Alarmed that this could ruin her plan, she suggested returning to their home, he on his motorbike and she following in the van. He agreed but demanded a kiss before leaving. She obliged and sent him to his death.

The murder of Leslie Hutchinson was a messy affair. Green estimated hitting him six or eight times with a lead-filled pipe before wrapping the belt around his mouth and neck. He then kicked him as he lay dying on the ground. A pathologist listed a dozen separate head wounds. Bigby said he had helped fix the wire but then froze as his business partner struggled vainly to recover from the shock attack.

Hutchinson had cried out during the struggle, his voice drifting to the caravan where his wife was waiting. She would later say he called to her "Get the police, Madge" as he fell under Green's blows. Crucially for the police, his cries were also heard by someone who had just stepped off a train at nearby Hessle Station. Although the man did not immediately connect the muffled sound he heard with an assault, he was able to help detectives pinpoint the exact time of the crime.

With Hutchinson now dead, Green returned to the caravan with his clothes covered in blood. After changing some of them and washing his blood-spattered face and hands, Mrs Hutchinson gave him three £5 notes and a roll of £1 notes, the money she would later tell police had been stolen from her husband's wallet.

Green and Bigby then carried the body to the side of the railway embankment, clumsily dragging it for some of the way and leaving more clues for the police in the process. All three then left he scene in Mrs Hutchinson's van.

As the two lovers put on a show of innocence at Hull Fair, Green returned home to wash again, burn his clothing and dispose of the murder weapon in a nearby bonfire. He also kicked off his shoes and carelessly abandoned them in a street.

Barely two hours after murdering a man he hardly knew, Green walked into the Portland Arms and ordered a whisky and a pint of bitter. After a second pint he ordered drinks all round and handed over a £5 note to pay for it, putting his seemingly sudden fortune down to a winning bet on the horses that afternoon. The licensee quickly realised he would not have been able to collect his winnings until the following day but Green said the money for the drinks was coming from his wages. He also asked for another £5 note to be changed at the bar because, he said, he didn't like them.

The police established from Green's employers that his wages that week had been in £1 notes while Leslie Hutchinson's had contained £5 notes. They also suspected, but were never able to prove, that the pieces of charred boot found in Mrs Hutchinson's fire had belonged to Bigby and had been burned after being covered in blood during the murder.

At the end of the week-long trial, Marjorie Hutchinson was found guilty of murdering her husband and was jailed for life. Roy Bigby was found not guilty but was sent to prison for three years after admitting a lesser charge of conspiracy to assault Leslie Hutchinson.

During four hours in the witness box, Mrs Hutchinson stuck by her claim that she had only intended her husband to receive a "good hiding". After unravelling her known lies to the police, the prosecution simply claimed she planned the killing to start a new life with her new boyfriend knowing she would pocket her husband's insurance money.

A final drama was the birth of her daughter a few months after starting her prison sentence. Mrs Hutchinson had been unknowingly pregnant by her husband as she plotted his death.

MURDERS OF HULL

BODY OF EVIDENCE

✝

They looked like something from a science fiction film, silhouetted against the sky dressed head to foot in black and wearing face masks. Each gloved hand held a spade and each rubber boot shifted uneasily on the ever-moving mountain of rubbish underneath. The head of Humberside CID, Detective Chief Superintendent John Crawley, said he had never dealt with a case like it in his career. The team of 30 officers searching the huge open refuse tip in Bransholme, which was home for most of Hull's domestic rubbish at the time, hoped they would never have to deal with one like it again.

Inoculated against tetanus, they were looking for the dismembered body of an 18-year-old girl which had been placed into plastic bags and then carried to the tip by an unsuspecting dustbin lorry. It was likely that somewhere on the tip was the dead girl's decapitated head.

The bags, together with the rest of the lorry's load, had been dumped there a month earlier. A mechanical excavator brought in to help the search was now digging down 15ft to move tons of rotting rubbish and mud onto wooden boards for the officers to sift through. Specialist body-seeking police dogs were soon withdrawn and the search team moved from one area of the tip to another, using discarded newspapers to give them clues as to when that particular pile of garbage had been dumped.

Eventually they gave up. Similar exhaustive and ultimately unsuccessful searches had been carried out in the Bradford and Shipley areas of West Yorkshire where some parts of the body were also thought to be hidden.

In any murder inquiry, prime importance is attached to the body, particularly for the wealth of evidence that comes with it. Without one, but with someone in custody admitting to cutting it up, this was to be an altogether different investigation. It was the murder inquiry that never was.

Before coming to Hull, Carol Rogers had spent most of her life in Dr Barnado's homes. Placed in care at the age of five, she lived in a home in Shipley until she turned 17 in 1978. Apart from a sister, her family had disintegrated. In the autumn of that year, Carol moved to Hull with her boyfriend, Ian Roberts, who also hailed from Shipley.

He had come to study computer sciences at Hull University and the young couple were able to rent a two bedroomed flat on Mizzen Road, off Beverley High Road, after Carol began working as a clerk with an insurance company.

Neighbours said they seemed a happy couple until one day the following January when Carol unexpectedly failed to turn up at work. Shortly afterwards, Roberts asked university officials to be re-housed on the campus and he was given a single room in one of the halls of residence. He said they had split up and promptly sold all the furniture from the flat to a second-hand dealer.

With still no sign of their colleague after the following weekend, two girls from the insurance office called round but found an empty flat. They assumed Carol and her boyfriend had simply moved on.

Roberts carried on with his studies as normal for nearly a month before confiding his terrible secret with a friend over a drink in the university bar. Advised by his shocked friend to tell the campus authorities, Roberts broke down and the police were called in. When he was finally interviewed at a solicitor's office in Hull, detectives could hardly believe what they were hearing.

The 20-year-old told them that he and Carol had quarrelled one morning in the flat over their wedding plans. Standing on the landing, he had grabbed her by the pyjamas and lifted her onto her toes.

He said she then fell over the staircase rail and landed head first at the bottom of the stairs. Apparently dead, he then threw a blanket over the body as two people walked past the front door on the verandah outside.

Roberts then detailed how he had been afraid to touch the body and instead decided to tie a clothes line around the neck and drag it back upstairs and into the bathroom. Once inside, he placed the body in the bath, slit the throat with a penknife and turned on the taps. He told amazed detectives that he knew how to drain the blood from dead animals from watching and helping his father, who worked as a butcher.

Leaving the body in the bath he thumbed a lift back to his parents' home in Shipley. The following day he returned to Hull in his father's car with a young friend, a 13-year-old boy, who was sent to a shop to buy some rubber gloves.

Roberts bought himself a saw and, with the boy occupied downstairs, he proceeded to hack the body of his girlfriend to pieces and place her limbs into four plastic bags and two cardboard boxes. The butcher's son then calmly threw two of the bags down a waste disposal chute at the flats.

Leaving the rest of the parcelled-up body behind, he then drove back to his parents and spent the weekend in Shipley planning his next move. He returned to Hull on the following Monday with three youths from his home town. Two more bags went down the chute while his friends helped collect Carol's clothing and other possessions. Unknown to them, two cardboard boxes placed into the car contained the larger parts of her dead body.

Dropping the boys off in Shipley, Roberts then took Carol's belongings to her sister in Bradford, telling her that she had left him. On the way back to his parents, the two cardboard boxes were dumped in a roadside skip.

After telling the police he loved the girl, Roberts was charged with manslaughter and with the rare offence of preventing the burial of a corpse. He had no previous convictions and seemed a model student, with no evident sign of mental illness.

Without the body and a post-mortem there was no way of knowing for certain the exact cause of death. This point led the trial judge, Mr Justice Smith, to direct a not guilty verdict on the manslaughter charge. With only one person's evidence to rely on, the judge ruled, it was impossible to know whether the intention to kill had been present in what might have been simply a "silly quarrel".

After facing a possible life sentence for manslaughter, Roberts was eventually jailed for three years for dismembering his lover.

Like the search party on the Bransholme tip, the detectives called out on the hunt for a body in a house in East Hull were unlikely to forget it in a hurry.

It was Christmas Day in 1976 and instead of tucking into a turkey dinner and unwrapping presents, the officers were uncovering the remains of a man who had been missing for over three years.

They arrived at the house on Holderness Road, near to East Park, after a dramatic Christmas Day confession at Hull's central police station. Early that morning, unemployed Allan Lawrence walked into the station and told how he had murdered a 20-year-old man called Geoffrey Middleton in July 1973. The body, he said, was still under the floorboards of a room occupied by retired hairdresser Bertram Holmes.

Holmes answered the door when the detectives arrived and when told of their suspicions he confirmed the spot, pointing to the rear of the room near to the television set. Lifting the floorboards they quickly located what was left of the body, which had been buried under bricks and cement in a grave about two-and-a-half-feet deep. Because of the condition of the corpse it took 11 hours to recover all the remains from the makeshift grave.

Although both 23-year-old Lawrence and now Holmes admitted killing Middleton and burying him under the floorboards, the police still needed to identify the body. Faced with conducting a post-mortem on a badly decomposed corpse, Home Office pathologist Dr Michael Green nevertheless managed to find a tattoo with the name 'Graham' on the right forearm exactly matching a tattoo Middleton had. In addition, a partial palm print was obtained which was later matched with the missing man.

Dark areas of staining to the skull were consistent with head injuries but two ligatures found around the neck suggested the cause of death. One was a piece of window cord wrapped twice around the neck and knotted, the other was a piece of lighting flex which had been double knotted.

Geoffrey Middleton was last seen by his mother in late July 1973 when he called at her home with Lawrence and Holmes to pick up his unemployment cheque which had arrived through the post. He occasionally stayed with his mother but most of the time lived in the Holderness Road flat with the two other men.

All three were homosexual and emotions between them were always fraught. Both Lawrence and Middleton had slept at different times with Holmes, who at 64 was old enough to be their grandfather and infact had a daughter of his own. The former hairdresser was an unlikely sexual svengali figure, having been forced to give up work a few years earlier because of arthritis.

Two days after calling for the cheque, Lawrence and Holmes visited Middleton's mother and said her son had apparently gone off with a stranger in a lorry to London. The news was not a surprise as he was something of a drifter and his family thought little of it until months began to pass by without any word or letter.

The second major cover-up carried out by the pair involved an outstanding court fine. A month before his disappearance, all three men had been in court charged with stealing a vehicle tax licence. Middleton was fined £10 and the penalty was duly paid off in weekly £1 amounts, both before and after he had supposedly vanished to London.

Four months after he was last seen or heard of, his family decided to report him missing. As a result, the police visited Holmes at the flat to question the old man about Middleton's last known movements. The sergeant was given a familiar story of Middleton heading for the capital and he left unaware that the man he was looking for had been right underneath him.

Holmes continued living in the flat for the next three years but Lawrence moved on, going to live and work in Oldham at a garage owned by Holmes' daughter and her husband. Once, when drunk, he told them he had killed someone in Hull but was then restrained by the couple from telephoning the police as they unwittingly thought he would simply make himself look foolish.

However, the murder continued to haunt him and, having returned to Hull, he finally decided to turn himself in. Lawrence told the police it had not been planned but admitted once telling Holmes that his one ambition was to murder someone and get away with it.

Holmes said Middleton's name was eventually suggested as the likely victim. On the night of his death, the three had quarrelled over Middleton's plan to burgle a shop. Holmes admitted getting upset, grabbing a hammer and striking the younger man twice on the head as he sat in a rocking chair. Holmes then sat on his legs as Lawrence throttled him with the cord and flex.

Both pleaded guilty to murder and were jailed for life. Holmes was 67 when he was sentenced, one of the oldest defendants in a Hull murder case this century. Passing sentence on what was a generally motiveless crime, Mr Justice Thesiger concluded: "This was a cold-blooded and pointless murder".

The man who led the police search in Holmes' flat was Detective Superintendent Ronald Sagar, then deputy head of Humberside's CID. To him it was nothing new for 11 years earlier, while still a detective sergeant in the old Hull City force, he had uncovered another hidden body in similar grisly circumstances.

Early on the morning of Wednesday July 7 1965, worried William Foxton called the police to report that his 17-year-old daughter Ada was missing. She had failed to return home after telling her parents that she was going out to a dance the previous night.

Later that same day, Sagar stood outside of a house in Dover Street in Hull with a uniformed constable waiting for their knocks on the front door to be answered. Acting on a tip-off, they wanted to see Frank Marritt, a 25-year-old unemployed welder who lived in the ground floor flat with his wife.

They had been contacted by a neighbour who had first heard and then witnessed a curious chain of events unfold in Marritt's flat next door. First she heard a sound like pots being knocked over, followed by the cries and sobs of a woman. The neighbour initially dismissed the noise as just another late night fight between Mr Marritt and his wife but glancing out of her own bedroom window directly down into their living room she saw his arm rising and falling, as if hitting something hidden from her view in the corner. Minutes later she heard a vigorous sweeping sound which was repeated a short while later.

That morning she saw a pair of Mr Marritt's trousers hanging on the washing line. Still baffled over the noises, she went out and saw the trousers had been washed from the knee downwards. The next surprise came when Mrs Marritt appeared at her door, apparently unmarked, asking to borrow a spade. Later a green blanket was hung over the Marritt's rear verandah window as if to block out the view from next door before a series of scraping noises began from behind the blanket. Later still, the neighbour and her husband watched puzzled as Mr Marritt carried out mud-filled coal bags from the verandah area and emptied them on the overgrown weed-covered back garden.

Sagar tried a bluff when Marritt finally appeared at the rear door, pretending to check on gas meters in the house to see if they had been broken into. They entered through the verandah and into the living room where Marritt answered some routine questions while the detective tried to spot anything unusual about the room itself. There was no obvious sign of a struggle having taken place but two flagstones on the verandah caught his eye. Both were just below the window and appeared to have damp patches around their edges while soil was lying near the window and the back door.

Marritt explained the soil away by saying he had been trying to clear weeds from outside the back door. He took the officers outside and showed them the overgrown garden where fresh earth was scattered between the weeds. Marritt also appeared to have three or four fresh cuts to his face which he said had been cuts from shaving.

The two policemen left but Sagar was suspicious. He said later: "Something about the house and Marritt did not seem correct. The living room was by no means clean and yet the general atmosphere seemed fresh. This atmosphere did not fit in and we were far from satisfied with the situation."

Within 30 minutes he was back, accompanied by a detective inspector, with instructions to carry out a thorough search of the flat and, in particular, the verandah. At first, Marritt denied ever touching the flagstones but as the smaller of the two slabs was lifted and pushed to one side the officers immediately saw the clay underneath had recently been disturbed. Marritt was trembling and in a sweat as the second slab revealed the same broken clay. As they began to move the clay from near the window he suddenly shouted out: "Don't go any further, there's a body under there!". After a further minute's digging, part of a girl's leg was uncovered.

Marritt first told the police he met the girl with a seaman in a pub the previous night, all three returning to his house in a taxi. As he slept in one room, a fight broke out in the other and when he went into the room the girl was lying dead on the floor. He then fought with the seaman who ran off. Marritt admitted burying her but only because he thought he would be blamed for her murder.

The story quickly changed. When the police said they intended checking at the pub he said they had actually met outside the pub. He also said only he and the girl had taken a taxi when officers suggested they would make similar checks with the taxi driver. In addition, he could only give the seaman's first name as Joe, claiming they had only met the day before.

Inside his oven, police found a handbag, a heavily bloodstained coat and a glove. The remains of a shoe and underwear belonging to the girl were found in the fire grate. The post-mortem on the body revealed 25 stab wounds to the neck, throat, chest and hands. The examination also showed a second attack had taken place after death featuring heavy blows to the head by a blunt instrument. Recovered from the house was a freshly-cleaned kitchen knife and a 2lb metal bed mattress bracket, which was later found to have traces of blood and scalp hair on it.

The police could find no seaman called Joe but they did discover that Marritt and Ada Foxton had been spotted together in the Spencer Arms on the night she disappeared. It was not the pub Marritt had spoken of earlier.

Ada had just turned 17 but was far from being a shy teenager. On the night of her death she had made love with a former boyfriend at his house before heading into the city centre where she was a well-known face in many pubs. Later, her ex-boyfriend said she told him she got no pleasure from flirting with men except to see them make fools of themselves.

In the Spencer Arms, Marritt had lied about her age to the licensee and later took fright when the police arrived, only to breath a sigh of relief when they proceeded to carry off a drunk.

He was charged with murder while his 19-year-old wife, Christine, was initially charged with being an accessory after the fact. The case against her was withdrawn at the committal hearing after the court was told she knew little or nothing about the murder. Mrs Marritt had actually left her husband the previous weekend, walking out after yet another row over his drinking and womanising. She was told the story about the seaman when she returned to the flat on the Wednesday morning and reluctantly went for a spade, telling her husband he should go to the police.

Marritt maintained his story at his trial but the jury at Leeds Assizes took just two hours to find him guilty. The prosecution suggested he had snapped while drunk, possibly as the teenager teased him in his bedroom.

Jailing Marritt for life, the judge, Mr Justice Havers, said the guilty verdict had been reached "on abundant evidence" and added: "It was a brutal and savage murder, one of the worst I have had the misfortune to come across".

THE FIREBUG

✝

n January 20 1981, a 20-year-old from Hull was ordered to be detained indefinitely at a special hospital after admitting killing 26 people during six years of undetected fire raising. In the course of one dramatic day at Leeds Crown Court, Bruce George Peter Lee had become the biggest mass killer in modern British criminal history. On paper at least, his catalogue of crime was shocking. Eleven separate fires claiming the lives of victims ranging from a six-month-old baby to a 95-year-old man.

The prosecution spoke of his "animal cunning" in describing how he continually managed to avoid suspicion for his terrible toll of death. Lee's own account to the police of how a tingling in his fingers signalled the need to start another blaze was every headline writer's dream.

Yet to the few people who could honestly say they knew something about Lee, the fact that he was standing in the dock at all was just as shocking. They knew him as 'Daft Peter', the simpleton with a limp and a semi-paralysed hand who had difficulty even striking a match.

Lee's case was one contradiction after another and in late 1983 he was cleared by the Court of Appeal of causing the deaths of 11 men at an old people's home in Hessle. The same court had earlier refused leave to appeal against all but three of the convictions against him. With the Wensley Lodge conviction quashed, his appeals in the other two cases were withdrawn. Unlike most serial killings, the fatal fires which Lee started were never linked until his confession. Remarkably, all but one were regarded as accidents by police and fire investigators and time after time inquests returned verdicts of misadventure. These findings were made to look even more premature when it was later revealed that Lee's technique was repeated over and over again. Not only were the attacks exclusively on occupied dwellings but they were almost always started with paraffin, usually by linking two pools of paraffin to create a 'fuse' to give himself time to get away.

The seeming random nature of his attacks gave no clues to the police that the fires were the work of one man. Curiously, all his victims had been incapacitated either by old age, extreme youth or disability but even after admitting them to police, detectives could only establish a motive in just four of the blazes and the grudges Lee held against these victims were at best described as trivial.

Born Peter Dinsdale, as a teenager Lee later changed his name by deed poll to emulate the Kung Fu film star featured in posters spread across his bedroom wall. It seemed his idol had everything he lacked — strength, respect, good looks and, above all, popularity.

He had never known his father, who left his mother Doreen shortly before his birth. Home life for Lee and his younger sister was anything but secure. Their mother worked as a prostitute, frequently disappeared leaving her children with relatives and went through two stormy marriages. Inevitably, the children were in and out of care homes and Lee also attended a special school in the city, being classed as borderline educationally sub-normal. His disabled hand and arm prevented him applying for the trawlerman's job he dreamed of as a boy and instead he drifted through a succession of training schemes. Odd jobs, such as helping out at speedway and rugby matches at Hull FC's Boulevard stadium, gave him extra money on top of the dole.

No-one could really class themselves as a close friend of the loner, who was regarded as stupid by some and egotistical by others. He spent what little money he had in pubs and amusement arcades. By the time he was 19, he was living with his mother in a maisonette flat off Cavill Place, a grim estate of concrete tower blocks which were already falling apart despite being only just over a decade old.

Often drunk, Lee rarely washed and wore filthy clothes. To some on the estate he was a frightening figure covered in crudely drawn tattoos, regularly threatening those who mocked him and once shaving off his hair with a razor blade for seemingly no reason.

In December 1979, a fatal house fire sent shockwaves through the city. Three young brothers — Charles, Peter and Paul Hastie — died from burns and injuries suffered in a blaze which swept through their Selby Street home. Firemen clearing the debris could smell paraffin despite the fact the council house had no paraffin heater or supplies of the fuel. Forensic scientists confirmed what the smell first suggested and detectives felt certain enough to state that inflammable liquid had probably been poured through the letterbox and set alight.

Their inquiry was not an easy one. It soon became clear that the Hastie family were not popular with some of their neighbours. Stories of feuds and vendettas began to fill the ears of policemen trudging the streets knocking on doors. An anonymous poison pen letter written a year earlier was found in the house threatening the family. The police even took the unusual step of commenting on the animosity they had encountered towards the family as well as pointing out the known disturbances caused by the Hastie children, which ranged from stone-throwing to fighting.

What they kept from the public was the fear that whoever was responsible for the fire might not only strike again, but could also have done exactly the same before.

The boys' father, Tommy, had been in prison at the time of the tragedy serving a sentence for a minor burglary offence. The jail term was later waived on compassionate grounds and he returned to be with his wife, Edith, who had escaped the fire, and their surviving four children.

Shortly after his release, the Hasties were invited to listen to a routine recording of a call made direct to the police operations room. The caller claimed responsibility for the boys' deaths and expressed his sorrow. When asked his name, he quickly rang off. Neither recognised the voice and there was no reason why they should, for they had never met Bruce Lee.

A week after the call, Lee put in an even more audacious appearance. Walking into a police station, he proceeded to give a witness statement about the fire saying he had overheard a man in a pub say he was responsible. The police rightly dismissed it as a pack of lies and Lee was forgotten about.

Gradually, the early momentum of the police inquiry began to wind down. The number of officers assigned to the case dwindled to a handful led by Supt Ronald Sagar, deputy head of Humberside CID. He knew months of exhaustive police work were in danger of coming to nothing when he left his office at the old Gordon Street station one Spring evening and went to look again at the boarded-up council house.

With no obvious suspect and most leads developed to the full without success, he decided to act on a hunch. The eldest Hastie boy, Charles, had been 15-years-old and was known to frequent amusement arcades. Sagar thought the youngster, like most boys of his age, could be experimenting with sex and he knew arcades were often used as a pick-up point by homosexuals.

For six weeks, the police staked out a public toilet near to Selby Street. Like many in the city, the toilet was known as a meeting place for homosexuals and young boys. A list of men and the boys they sought out for paid sex was drawn up and in May 1980 Lee was among a number of young men to be questioned by the police.

He had been introduced to homosexuality while in care and when quizzed about Charles Hastie he admitted knowing the youngster but gave little else away. Until then the police were concentrating on a theory that the arson attack had actually been meant for the house of a drug dealer who lived next door to the Hasties. A month later, Sagar instructed the toilet 'suspects' to be brought back to the station for questioning. Lee was arrested in a city centre amusement arcade but was too drunk to be questioned immediately and he was left to sober up in a cell.

At the time Sagar had no reason to suspect Lee or any of the other men of the Hastie fire but he adopted the same tactic as each one sat down in front of him, immediately suggesting they had been responsible. One of the last to be seen, Lee was dealt with in the same way as the others and in reply to Sagar's first question simply said: "I didn't mean to do it".

That answer unlocked the case and the detective leading the seven-month inquiry breathed a sigh of euphoric relief as he realised from Lee's muffled speech that he was the same person who had left the anonymous message taped in the operations room immediately after the fire. By the early hours of the next morning, Lee had given enough details about the fire which had been kept from the public that the police were confident they had found the Hasties' killer.

During the interview Lee said he carried out the attack because he was sick of the boy always asking for money after committing indecent acts with him. His seeming lack of remorse nagged at Sagar's instincts and two weeks later he visited Lee at Armley Jail in Leeds to test his suspicions. Within hours Lee had confessed to starting two more fires, one of them fatal.

A series of 20 detailed interviews with Lee were carried out by Sagar during the following week and slowly but surely the other fires were admitted. His confessions staggered the police, who had to re-open their files on fires previously written off as accidents.

As the prosecution said at Lee's trial, the interviews represented a slow, painstaking creation of confidence between Sagar and Lee. The detective later spoke of his astonishment at Lee's ability to recall minute details about incidents while Lee began to see his interrogator as the first person in his life he could trust. While on remand, Lee asked for a Bible and when given one by Sagar proceeded to quote from Matthew, Chapter Six, in answer to why he had started so many fires. Verse 24 says: "No man can be a slave to two masters," and adds that if a man does have two masters, he should despise one but be devoted to the other. In his statement to the police, Lee claimed devotion to fire and hatred of people.

The blazes he confessed to make gruesome reading. In one, a man died in a fireball at his home which at the time had been attributed to sparks from an open grate catching the man's clothing as he slept. Lee said he had poured paraffin over the sleeping man before setting him alight after they earlier argued about the man's racing pigeons. Another fire which killed a six-year-old boy was thought to have been started by a gas leak while the death of an 82-year-old woman was initially put down to her habit of smoking in bed.

But Lee's most shocking — and as it turned out controversial — confession concerned the fire which killed 11 elderly men at the Wensley Lodge old people's home in Hessle in January 1977.

He told police he had cycled to the home, kicked in a window, climbed a flight of stairs and started a fire using paraffin in the bedroom of a sleeping 75-year-old man. His explanation for burning down Wensley Lodge was that he simply wanted to set fire to a large house that night. Until then the area's worse blaze for 30 years had always been regarded as a tragic accident.

An inquest jury returned a misadventure verdict on all the dead victims and an independent committee of inquiry confirmed their view that the fire had almost certainly been started by heat from a plumber's blow torch.

On the afternoon of the fire, a plumber was working in the boiler room directly under the room where Lee was later to claim he had first lit his paraffin. The inquiry found that during soldering work to a pipe only inches from the ceiling, the blowtorch had ignited fireboard and a joist between the ceiling and the floor of the room above. It smouldered undetected for five hours until it reached a vertical duct behind the bedroom walls. When smoke in the corridors finally alerted staff, the room door was opened and a so-called 'flashover fire' erupted as the fresh oxygen from outside reacted with the flames.

While on remand, nothing could shake Lee from going back on his confessions to the police, most of which were either given without the presence of a solicitor as he had refused to see one or against his solicitor's advice to say nothing. He even seemed to relish his fate, allegedly telling police: ''Those 26 are going to put me in the Guiness Book of Records''.

At his trial, Lee pleaded guilty to 26 separate offences of manslaughter and 11 cases of arson. The prosecution accepted his pleas of not guilty to 26 cases of murder on the grounds of diminished responsibility, taking the view that the public interest did not demand a full trial and that justice could be done by accepting Lee's pleas.

A month after being ordered to be detained ''without limit'' in a mental hospital, Lee wrote to his solicitors asking them to mount an appeal. In November 1983 he told the Court of Appeal that his confessions to the police had been untrue. Giving his first ever public evidence since his arrest three years earlier, Lee said he lied to avoid further police questioning, signed statements he could barely read and picked pleas which would ensure that he was sent to a hospital rather than jail.

His interrogator, Det Supt Sagar, also gave evidence saying Lee had seemed relieved rather than confused when making his confession. The detective also rejected suggestions of a breach in the procedures laid down for interviews with prisoners.

Leave to appeal was refused in all but three of the cases. A month later the Appeal Court quashed his convictions for manslaughter and arson at Wensley Lodge after deciding that forensic evidence against Lee was ''unsatisfactory''.

The three Appeal Court judges went out of their way to praise the way Sagar had both handled the interviews and obtained Lee's confessions but they were scathing about Home Office forensic scientist Graham Daveport.

In the 1977 committee of inquiry into the Wensley Lodge fire Mr Daveport gave expert evidence supporting the blowtorch theory. But after hearing Lee's confession, he changed his mind and concluded it had been arson by the use of paraffin.

Lord Justice Ackner said this change of view underlined the "inadequate investigation" Mr Daveport had carried out into the fire. This meant the court could not rule out the possibility that the fire was an accident and, as a result, the judges ruled that Lee had to be given the benefit of the doubt.

Lord Justice Ackner said Lee could have easily learned about the fire and fantasised his part in it to revel in the publicity it would bring.

In a 1985 newspaper interview, Ron Sagar attempted to put the record straight once and for all after a series of critical articles in the Sunday Times focused on his handling of the Lee inquiry.

"No-one feels more sorry for Lee than me and why anyone should think we would want to pin on him deaths that were already recorded as accidental is beyond me," he said.

Two years later he won an undisclosed five-figure sum in damages after an out-of-court settlement over a libel action he mounted against the Sunday Times over the articles.

Today, with 15 manslaughter convictions still to his name, Bruce Lee remains Britain's biggest convicted mass killer.

FATAL ATTRACTION

✝

It was the sort of night when it was easy to forget there was a war on — a busy Sunday evening in a Hessle Road club, packed full of laughter, music and good cheer. Hull had survived Hitler's Blitz the previous year but at a terrible cost. Hundreds had died or had suffered serious injury and parts of the city had been reduced to rubble. Bombing raids were still very much a nightly threat and as the clubgoers drank away their worries, the last batch of 60 orphans from Newland Homes were preparing to be evacuated to the relative calm of the countryside at Pately Bridge.

Among the happy throng in the club were James Roberts, a corporal in the Army, and his girlfriend, Dorothy Gardiner. Leaving after time had been called, they walked home hand-in-hand through blacked-out streets which were pock-marked with damaged buildings from previous bomb blasts. Rows of terraced homes had holes punched in them where families had once lived.

As they walked along a 10-foot between Hessle Road and the Boulevard, the opened wooden doors of a garage partially blocked their path. As the garage appeared disused Cpl Roberts peered inside as he drew closer. It was a cold but clear March night, lit up by a full moon and what he saw caused an extra chill to run up his spine.

On the garage floor was something white. It was either a pile of bricks and mortar or a body. Fearing the worst, he persuaded his girlfriend it was the former but suggested she should stay outside while he investigated. Left alone, he touched whatever it was with his foot and immediately knew his suspicions had been correct. The body was covered in blood and stains also speckled the garage walls.

The soldier came outside and calmly escorted his girlfriend back onto Hessle Road where he met two Army friends. They quickly returned to the scene, striking matches inside the garage to confirm Cpl Roberts' grim discovery. within minutes the police had arrived.

There was nothing at the scene to immediately identify who the dead girl was. She appeared to be a teenager and money lay scattered about on the floor. Her clothes, which included a three-quarter length navy blue coat and a green cotton dress, appeared to have been torn from the neck down to her waist but there was no evidence of any sexual assault. The head injuries which had killed her were caused by a broken and bloodstained fireside kerb which had been found lying across her throat.

Weighing just over three stone, the tiled kerb had come from a nearby blitzed property and was being stored in the garage. The police knew this unusual murder weapon could only have been used by someone who was exceptionally strong. They also found bruises to her eye and mouth probably caused by punches. The likely scenario was of the girl being punched in the face, falling to the floor probably unconscious and then being struck on the head with the kerb. Because of its weight, the police believed it had been deliberately laid over her throat rather than dropped from a height at the end of the assault.

Although the girl carried no identity, the police did not have to wait long to find out who she was. Alice Hague had gone to the police after her 14-year-old daughter had failed to return home from running an errand to the corner shop. Instead of reporting her missing, Mrs Hague was told she had been murdered.

The war had brought grief and joy to Alice Hague. Her common-law husband, a bos'un on the Hull steam trawler Luceda, had died two years earlier in 1940 when the vessel struck a mine in the North Sea and was lost with all hands. Pregnant at the time, she later gave birth to a daughter.

Her eldest daughter Alice Ann took her father's surname. At 14 she looked slightly older than her age and was already working at Linsley's beer-bottling store in Dagger Lane. On Sunday, March 1, 1942, she had been to the cinema and arrived back at her Constable Street home at about 8.30pm when her mother asked her to run an errand to buy cigarettes and candles. It was the last time Mrs Hague saw her daughter alive.

Alice Widdowson had no luck at the shop but she wasn't in any rush to return home empty-handed. Young boys who knew her later told police they saw her walking arm-in-arm with a youth who had called out her name as he stood at the corner of the Boulevard where it meets Hessle Road. One of the boys who had talked to Alice earlier that night recalled how she had been boasting about her boyfriends, not just one but three and all aged in their early 20s.

"I shall be losing you when I come back as I am going to meet my bloke," she told one of the boys as she headed for the shop. Another youngster said of her: "She would go out with almost anybody."

Within 24 hours the police had sufficient evidence from eyewitnesses to release a detailed description of Alice's "bloke". He was aged about 17-years-old, standing 5ft 5ins tall, and of medium build. At the time he was wearing a fawn overcoat with a vent at the back, dark trousers and dark shoes. Unusually for the fashions of the day, witnesses recalled he was not wearing a hat.

Alice's body had been found within a few hundred yards of her home and detectives were convinced her killer had very detailed local knowledge of the area. Why else would her attacker have chosen a disused garage behind an unoccupied bomb-damaged house to carry out the assault, making sure that if she did scream she would not be heard?

Her mother was asked about Alice's boyfriends but could not say she knew of a regular suitor. All she knew was that her daughter had been anxious to find a job after leaving school.

Three days after the grim discovery of Alice Widdowson's death, another teenager's body was found in an air raid shelter in nearby St George's Road.

A police reservist had been called to the shelter at the rear of the house at 6.30am that morning to find the body of Derek Rose lying on a bunk with the smell of gas choking what little air there was to breathe. A post mortem would later reveal death had probably occurred some six hours earlier, the cause being recorded as asphyxia due to gas poisoning.

The reservist, Charles Howlett, emerged from the shelter expecting to offer comfort and sympathy to the boy's parents but instead found that neither seemed very shocked or upset by the tragedy. All the father seemed to want to say was that he had borrowed the gas stove which had been in the shelter. "I was greatly shocked at the lack of concern by both parents," Howlett said later.

For the officers investigating the Widdowson murder, the news was both a tragedy and a breakthrough. Although his parents steadfastly claimed he had spent the entire Sunday night at home with them, Rose was identified by at least three witnesses as having stood waiting on the corner of the Boulevard that night shortly before others saw Alice Widdowson hurrying to her rendezvous. Rose had even told one witness he was waiting for a girl.

The police also discovered that Rose had once lived directly opposite the girl in Constable Street, moving house when the family home had been destroyed during an air raid but not before he had taken Alice on a date to the cinema.

At 19, he was five years older than her and not afraid of chasing girls. Two who later gave evidence at his inquest claimed the apprentice bricklayer was full of cheek. One said he would not hesitate to use violence to get his way with a girl, the other recalled an incident when he nearly molested her in an office before she ordered him out.

Despite extensive enquiries, the police could not find anyone who had seen the teenagers together that night. But in schoolboy James Jordan and his uncle, Royal

Artillery gunner George Drew, they had two witnesses with compelling evidence.

Jordan had known Rose for about five years but had not expected a sudden visit from his friend, not once but twice that Sunday night. On the first occasion, at about 8.20pm, he called at the boy's home in the Boulevard to ask for the address of his brother. Over an hour later he returned, this time out of breath and asking for a drink of water. Explaining he had been running for a bus Rose then picked up a brush and cleaned mud off his overcoat which Jordan had pointed out.

The following night Rose again called at the house asking for the same address as before. George Drew, who did not like Rose, wrote it down and casually asked if he had heard abut the murder of Alice Widdowson. Rose said he knew the girl but seemed keen to leave. Before he went, he asked them that if his mother came "snooping around" they should tell her he had been with them all Sunday night. His excuse for the cover-up story was that he had been drinking that evening against his mother's wishes.

Another crucial witness was Cecil Adams, a foreman who was Rose's boss. he said the teenager was among the strongest young lads he had ever known with a quick-fire temper to match. A day before he was found dead, Adams had suggested he should try for the Commandos with his call-up looming but Rose replied: "I don't care what I go in. I am a dying man now and I shall be dead in six months."

The forensic evidence linking Rose to the murder was analysed in Wakefield and all pointed to the same conclusion. Fibres found on the girls' shoes matched Rose's coat, wool fibres on her clothing were consistent with his scarf and a female hair found under the arm of his coat also matched Alice Widdowson's dark brown hair. In both of his trouser pockets there were small human blood smears as if someone with grazed knuckles had placed their hands inside. A bloodstained handkerchief was found in one of the pockets and the brush used at James Jordan's house also had fibres which matched Rose's coat.

Although Hessle Road gossip immediately linked the two deaths the police could not officially do the same. Indeed three days after the discovery of Rose's body, as the funeral of Alice Widdowson was taking place in the Western Cemetery, Hull's Chief Constable Thomas 'Tosh' Wells was still reluctant to divulge anything to the Press. "I think we can say that interesting results in our murder inquiries are imminent," he announced to reporters. The Hull Daily Mail told its readers that a "definite line of inquiry" was said to be "developing satisfactorily". Details of Rose's death had yet to be released.

The unwillingness of the police to make their suspicious knows before an inquest was understandable. At the time, an inquest jury could return a verdict of wilful murder and it was open to them to identify Rose as the murderer.

Less than a month after the double tragedy this is exactly what they did. An open verdict was returned on Rose after being advised to do so by the coroner, Dr Norman Jennings. No suicide note had been found in the air raid shelter while tests had found no fault with the gas stove.

Chief Constable Wells took charge of presenting the case on behalf of the police and revealed Rose had secretly withdrawn his Post Office savings the day after Alice Widdowson's battered body had been found. A colourful character with a domineering personality, Wells also took the opportunity to put the youth's family on the spot over their continued claims that he had spent the night of the murder with them, playing ludo and listening to the radio.

In a sometimes heated exchange, he even sought to shoot holes in evidence given by the boy's grandmother that she had given him toast and cheese the night before he died. Wells knew the post mortem showed Rose had not eaten anything for at least 24 hours and promptly told the court.

His parents and even his 11-year-old brother testified that Rose never left the house but Wells' fierce questioning had been worthwhile. After the jury returned their unanimous verdicts, Dr Jennings decided the matter could not rest there. "The whole of the evidence in this case by the Rose family is going to the Director of Public Prosecutions," he announced. "To my mind they have committed perjury and the police have been humbugged from start to finish."

The inquest left several unanswered questions, not least why the police had failed to track down Rose, a seemingly obvious suspect, in the two days after the murder and before his own death. It also proved that like marriage, love affairs can end in tragedy.

Over 40 years later, love blinded a 50-year-old bachelor to such a degree that he meticulously planned a double funeral service to start a new life in paradise with the woman of his dreams. The case of the virgin and the vice girl shocked even hardened detectives who thought they had seen and heard everything in their job.

Cyril Olsen was an unlikely killer. Shy, quietly spoken and conscious of his 20-stone frame, he was a devoted only son who had lived with his parents all his life. Their deaths, within four months of each other in 1986, plunged him into a suicidal fit of depression.

His father, Alf, raced greyhounds at Craven Park and over the years Olsen also became a familiar figure at meetings. An acknowledged form expert, he was one of the few punters able to influence the odds simply by staking his own money on a dog. He also gambled on horse racing and struck lucky in 1982, a year after being made redundant, when he scooped £20,000 on a winning double bet.

But with the sudden loss of his elderly parents, the safe and secure world he had always known began to fall apart. He was about to enter a far darker one.

Olsen's grief took a grip on his reality. Despite inheriting a large amount of money to add to his own redundancy pay-out and the winnings from the bookies, he was only interested in joining his parents in the after-life he passionately believed in. Holding him back was the fact that he was still a virgin.

Being jilted by a teenage sweetheart when he was 18 and just about to enter National Service had scarred him deeply. Thirty-three years later while on trial for murder, he told a hushed court: "It shattered me. I never recovered from that and still think of her to this day."

Turning to his thoughts after his parents' death, he went on: "I had had no sexual experience. I did not even know what a woman looked like but I did not want to die a virgin, it was not manly. I was going to kill myself and I thought that before I go I will break my duck. At the time I weighed 20 stones, I was too timid, too shy. The only way I could meet a girl was on the street." That girl was prostitute Christine Acey and the street was Waterhouse Lane, in the heart of Hull's red light area. Olsen was about to discover that gambling was not the only vice in the world.

The streetwise mother-of-four was the exact opposite of the naive bachelor. She sold sex, took hard drugs and mixed freely with the city's criminal underworld. No stranger to the police, she carried out her business in a rented flat and used her takings to feed a long-term heroin habit. Once she was admitted to a special short-stay ward for drug users at Hull Royal Infirmary but discharged herself to return to the streets.

Embarrassed about his weight, Olsen said the prostitute was "kind and tried to help" during their first encounter.

Importantly for him, she did not laugh as he undressed. "I realised very quickly I was falling for her," he said later. But it was to be a fatal attraction. As he began to open his heart and his wallet, Acey started an affair with his money.

As they started to meet regularly, Olsen believed he was no longer just another client but her boyfriend. In fact she continued to live with her common-law husband, the father of two of her children. Whenever Olsen visited her Ellerby Grove home in East Hull, her husband pretended to be her brother.

Over a 10-month period the besotted bachelor spent an incredible £25,000 on the woman he fondly called Chris. Furniture, carpets, a washing machine and new clothes were among his gifts, along with a £900 diamond encrusted gold watch which was later sold behind his back. He also forked out £4,000 for a fortnight's holiday in the Canary Islands for Acey and one of her girlfriends.

He also handed over large amounts of cash, primarily to feed her heroin addiction. At first, Olsen tried to persuade her to take heroin-substitute drugs such as methadone but her craving demanded more. By the time she was desperately injecting heroin into veins in her groin, he was even using heroin himself in a futile bid to cement their relationship. At his trial, the jury heard that he once gave her nearly £1,000 in cash to buy half-an-ounce of heroin from a newly-arrived consignment of the drug in Hull. He was told to expect a £2,000 profit on 'wraps' of the drug being sold on the street at £20 a time. Typically, he never saw a penny as it was alleged Acey and her friends simply sold half, kept the money and used the remaining heroin themselves. The gentle giant with no previous criminal record of any kind was now shedding weight because of his own drugs habit and losing hundreds of pounds in sterling in the process.

With his own money running out, he began to fear losing everything. He was no longer the 'sugar daddy' who could wave his cheque book like a magic wand. Acey had begun to avoid him and his Upavon Garth home in Bransholme suddenly suffered a series of break-ins. Reluctantly, he faced the prospect of her returning to prostitution to pay the bills. "I hated the thought of her going back on the streets. In the time I knew her, Chris had become like a wife and no wife of mine could sell herself on the streets," he would say later. "I thought she deserved a better life. I thought 'We will go together. It will get her off the streets, off drugs, into paradise.' That was when I decided to kill myself. Once I decided to do it I was at peace."

Olsen made elaborate preparations for his planned trip to paradise with the drug-taking prostitute by his side. In a series of notes found later to friends, relatives and neighbours, he provided precise details for a double funeral, including a procession along Hessle Road where they both grew up, and a strict request that no hymns be sung. Instead, he wanted a tape recording of his mother's own funeral service played.

One note spelled out his feelings. "Life is not worth living without Christine. I am seeing less of her and it is tearing me apart." He even wrote out a joint obituary notice saying "We shall be reunited in paradise — we will walk hand-in-hand in the land of dreams."

Christine Acey lay asleep when the first of 32 hammer blows struck her head. Olsen had kept the tool under his pillow ever since the spate of burglaries at his home. After knocking her unconscious, he then suffocated her with a pillow, held her head under bath-water before wrapping the horrific head wounds in a towel and laying her body back in bed.

However his quest for self-proclaimed paradise was shattered when his own suicide attempt failed. Despite taking a massive overdose of more than 150 painkillers and sleeping tablets, Olsen woke up alive. Even then he thought of jumping off the Humber Bridge but, instead, collapsed yards from his home in a vain attempt to walk there.

When he appeared at York Crown Court nearly a year later charged with murder he looked a shadow of the roly-poly figure so familiar to his old friends at Craven Park. He had lost nearly 10 stones and looked gaunt and thin-faced.

It was revealed that at the time of his arrest he had just £200 left in the bank. Despite damning evidence of being manipulated by Acey and her friends, he refused to condemn her. "I still love her just as I loved her before," he told the court. "I have a picture of her at home and when my time comes I have asked this to go into the coffin with me. That will help me meet her again."

After evidence was submitted by both sides, the prosecution decided not to ask the jury to contemplate a guilty verdict on the murder charge. The judge, Donald Herrod QC, said the move was "very right and very fair" before formally instructing the jury to find Olsen guilty of manslaughter on the grounds of diminished responsibility. Medical evidence suggested the infatuated bachelor was severely depressed at the time and could not tell right from wrong. He was jailed for seven years.